The Turner Report

The Turner Report

Randy Turner

iUniverse, Inc.
New York Lincoln Shanghai

The Turner Report

iUniverse books may be ordered through booksellers or by contacting:

iUniverse
2021 Pine Lake Road, Suite 100
Lincoln, NE 68512
www.iuniverse.com
1-800-Authors (1-800-288-4677)

Because of the dynamic nature of the Internet, any Web addresses or links contained in this book may have changed since publication and may no longer be valid.

The views expressed in this work are solely those of the author and do not necessarily reflect the views of the publisher, and the publisher hereby disclaims any responsibility for them.

ISBN: 978-0-595-46750-1 (pbk)
ISBN: 978-0-595-91045-8 (ebk)

Printed in the United States of America

Contents

FOREWORD

During the seven and a half years I served as managing editor of the *Lamar Democrat* (1982 to 1990) one of my favorite pastimes on cold, rainy weekends was to go upstairs in the Democrat building and examine old copies of the newspaper, some dating back as far as 1867, 16 years before it took the name *Lamar Democrat*.

I always took special care when turning the pages, since some were so brown and brittle with age that they literally crumbled if treated as you would treat a normal newspaper.

My favorite time period to research, without question, was the nearly half a century (1900 to 1948) when the newspaper was published and edited by Arthur Aull, an era that Missouri Southern State University professor Chad Stebbins evoked brilliantly in his book, *All the News is Fit to Print: Profile of a Country Editor*. As older Lamar residents, or those who have read Stebbins' book know, there was no aspect of small-town life that Arthur Aull did not memorialize in the pages of his newspaper. Like most other newspapers of that era (and this one), Aull would print every detail of murder investigations or fatal car accidents, or damaging storms. Unlike nearly every other newspaper in existence, Aull also printed every detail of every divorce case that was heard in a Barton County courtroom. And there were times when Lamar residents, not thrilled to see their peccadilloes revealed to the Democrat readership, took out their frustration on Aull, and not just by writing letters to the editor.

Reading those old newspapers gave me a feeling for the town, its people, and its history, something extremely important for a newcomer. It also gave me the opportunity to add historical perspective to my writing.

When I left the *Democrat* to work for *The Carthage Press* in April 1990, I was fortunate enough to have three members of the news staff who had considerable experience in the community and helped me develop not only knowledge of the town, but also of The Press—Managing Editor Neil Campbell, City Editor Jack Harshaw and Marvin VanGilder. The Press also had back issues, also dating back to the 19th century, on its third floor, and I read those whenever I had a chance.

But in the eight years since the newspaper business left me (and I will leave that story for a future book), I have watched as that institutional history has vanished at The Press and at other newspapers in southwest Missouri and, in fact, across the nation. Each new story is treated as if nothing like it has ever happened before. It is information without context, knowledge without understanding.

When I decided to follow my two novels with a collection of stories I covered during my newspaper days, my first step was to go through boxes and drawers full of clippings, old notebooks, and correspondence. But having written more than 20,000 articles during that time, I no longer have much of anything except the highlights of those years. So after I gathered all of the material I had in my apartment and in the attic at my parents' home in Newtonia, Missouri, I called *The Carthage Press*, the newspaper I worked for during most of the stories in this volume and asked if I could go through the back issues to help refresh my memory and perhaps add some information to the stories. Unfortunately, in the move from that three-story building in the heart of downtown Carthage to a much smaller building on Central Avenue, The Press no longer has back issues at its facility. I could go to the Carthage Public Library and look up old papers on microfilm, I was told. I thanked the kind lady who helped me, and I was prepared to go to the public library, but as it turned out I had *The Carthage Press* materials for the stories I included in this book,. It created no inconvenience for me, but it saddened me to think of a young reporter on a cold, rainy weekend not having access to the richest source of history available—the back issues of his newspaper. And young reporters in Carthage today do not have Neil Campbell, Jack Harshaw, and Marvin VanGilder in the news room to steer them in the right direction.

Times have changed.

This book features stories from my journalism career, but also some up-to-date investigative reporting of the type that I have featured in my blog *The Turner Report* for the past four years.

Hopefully, this book will bring back memories for readers who are familiar with these stories, while providing them with never-before-published information, provide some background material to add context to events that are happening today, and remind today's journalists that, contrary to what you see in your newspapers and hear on your broadcasts, and no matter what your editors say, you don't have to be boring to report the news.

TERROR ON THE MIDNIGHT SHIFT

When the light turns yellow—stop.

That was what I always told myself when I went through Webb City during the early 1990s. At one time, Webb City was primarily regarded as a suburb bedroom community, a town of approximately 7,500, most of whom made the daily trek to Joplin just a few miles away for work and then returned each evening.

As the '90s continued, Webb City became known for its string of state championship football teams, a string that has continued into the 21st century. But in the early 1990s, the city also had a reputation as a town with a few rogue police officers who enjoyed making the most of the power they held over those who were unfortunate enough to cross their path.

And I was one of those who crossed their path—deliberately.

It was early November 1990 as I traveled east through Webb City, nine miles away from the Jasper County seat, Carthage, where I worked as the area reporter for The Carthage Press.

To get through Webb City, you had to go through three stoplights. I had just gone through the first one, when I saw a black-and-white police cruiser crossing lanes to pull in behind me.

Normally, I would not have been nervous. I had only had one traffic violation, a speeding ticket in Cedar County in 1988 in 15 years, and I was breaking no traffic laws. I made sure of that. I checked the speedometer; I was five miles below the limit. Still, my heart was pounding a mile a minute. If this police officer knows who I am, he's going to pull me over. I glanced at my watch, it was ten minutes before 1 a.m. The midnight shift was on. And in Webb City, Missouri, that meant trouble.

Unfortunately, my timing was off as we approached the second traffic signal. It was green, but I could tell it was just about to change. Normally, I would have plenty of time, but if it changed at the wrong moment, and I continued through the intersection, I would probably be pulled over and if they found out who I was, I could be in for a beating.

The light was still green, and the officer was right behind me. I saw the light turning to yellow. Should I stop? I asked myself. If I did, I was probably going to have a police officer ramming the back end of my car, so I said a silent prayer and zipped on through, the officer right behind me. So far, he had not turned on his light. Maybe I was going to make it. Then he pulled up right beside me, where he stayed for a long, uncomfortable few seconds that seemed more like hours.... and then the lights began flashing. He had me. I pulled over onto the shoulder ... and watched as he sped right past me, pursuing some actual lawbreaker.

The officer pulled into the right-hand lane and turned in to the Take-a-Break convenience store at the third stoplight, where another police officer had a motorist stopped. I breathed a deep sigh of relief, continued to travel well under the speed limit and headed home.

In retrospect, it seems silly to think that I feared being pulled over for something like that. But those were not normal times for The Carthage Press or for the Webb City Police Department, and things were not going to be normal for years to come.

◆   ◆   ◆

At the time of what I thought of as my near-miss in Webb City, I had been the area reporter for The Carthage Press for only seven months, a somewhat older than usual rookie reporter at a daily newspaper. My only experience at a daily had been 12 years earlier when I was sports editor at the Lamar Democrat. That job lasted only eight months. In between, my journalism experience was limited to weekly newspapers, and there were a lot of people who thought I was going to fall flat on my face when I decided to make the switch when I was already in my mid-30s.

And there was no one who was scared of failure more than I was. My first few months at Carthage were nothing special. I mainly covered area city council and school board meetings, did the occasional feature, and filled in for reporters on their days off or when all of the reporters were assigned to other stories. One thing Managing Editor Neil Campbell learned quickly was that I wanted to work. I was never a person who was comfortable with down time. When I finished with one story, I was ready to work on the next.

But after my first six months at The Press, I had yet to land one story that really challenged me. That was about to change in October 1990. Ironically, considering that I later built a reputation for breaking big stories, I had nothing to do with breaking the one that ended up making my reputation in Carthage.

That honor belonged to Andy Ostmeyer, a reporter with the area's biggest newspaper, the Joplin Globe. It was Ostmeyer who wrote the story of a man named Vince McCarty from nearby Carterville, who was pulled over on a bad check warrant by an officer from the Webb City Police Department's midnight shift. McCarty later claimed he had been severely beaten by three officers while he was in the Webb City Jail. Ostmeyer, a skilled reporter and gifted communicator, broke the story and it was the talk of Jasper County. And The Carthage Press did not have anything on it. I later learned that the information had been brought to Ostmeyer. Nothing wrong with that. He had earned his reputation and though he was younger than I was, the people who wanted to make the Webb City Police pay for Vince McCarty's beating, had no reason to think of me or The Press when they decided to go to public.

As I read Ostmeyer's gripping account of the Vince McCarty story, I knew I had to get in on this, and by a lucky twist of fate I did. One of my regular beats was Webb City's municipal government and a 6:30 p.m. Monday City Council meeting was scheduled for the next week. The agenda was light, just a few items before the council went into a closed session to discuss personnel matters. It was October, and it was stuffy in the ancient city building, so many of those at the meeting went outside and stood on the sidewalk while the council conferred in a meeting room inside.

I have never been a social person. I always stood on the outer perimeter and listened, and one talent I picked up early in my journalism career was the ability to pick out a conversation from several feet away and listen to it no matter how many distractions there were or how many other conversations were taking place.

On this night, the most interesting conversation revolved around the beating of Vince McCarty. Everyone was talking about Andy Ostmeyer's article. I heard one man say, "It sounds like they beat the hell out of him."

A woman answered, "You should hear the tape."

The tape? I leaned in closer and said, "I wouldn't mind hearing that tape."

The woman looked at me and quickly put me in my place.

"And who in the hell are you?"

Now that any illusions I had of the fame that comes with a career in journalism had been shattered, I meekly said, "I'm Randy Turner. I'm a reporter for The Carthage Press."

She paused for several long seconds, then said, "If you come to the Take-A-Break after 2:30 tomorrow, I'll have a copy of the tape for you." I agreed and in just those few seconds I had somehow managed to jump into the story of Vince McCarty's beating.

After about 15 minutes, the city council returned from its closed session, not that I cared. I was far more excited about the tape and anxious to get hold of a copy of it.

When the next day arrived, I was not going to give the woman the opportunity to back out of the agreement. I arrived at the Take-A-Break just before 2:30, and true to her word she had a copy of the tape for me.

The cassette player in my car was not working, so I had to drive back to Carthage and play it at the Press office. As I listened, it was hard to make out a lot of the words, but enough of them came through loud and clear. I had no doubt this tape was made at the Webb City Jail and that the beating of Vince McCarty had been captured. I still had questions though that needed to be answered. Had anything been edited out of the tape? Who were the people whose voices I heard? Were they the ones who had been mentioned in Ostmeyer's article? How did this tape come to exist in the first place? Why would someone secretly tape the Webb City Police Department? And, of course, the main question that a reporter always has during circumstances like this? Is my editor going to let me run this story?

◆   ◆   ◆

Before I talked to my editor, Neil Campbell, I did my best to verify the authenticity of the tape. I identified the voices with the help of a city council member, a city hall employee, and an officer from the Webb City P. D. day shift.

I still had not answered all of my questions, but I had enough to take the tape to Neil Campbell and get his reaction. It boiled down to one word. "Wow!"

After a short silence, Neil added, "We need to take this to Jim." Jim Farley was the publisher. When he listened, it was obvious he was getting a kick out of his newspaper having this tape. "This is great stuff," he said after we listened to it, "but we can't run it."

I had halfway expected this response, but I was still disappointed. I supposed I had been hoping that we would run with it without having it thoroughly checked out. It was the right decision … but maybe there was another way to approach it.

"The FBI has a copy of this tape," I told Jim and Neil, repeating what the woman at the convenience store told me.

"I'm listening," Jim said.

"I have a source at the FBI. If I can get him to confirm that they are looking at this tape …"

"And you're sure they have the same tape as the one you have?"

"According to both of the people I talked to."

"If you can get a confirmation from the FBI that they're looking into the tape and that it's the same tape, then we run with it."

"I'll see what I can do."

Twenty minutes later, I had my confirmation and thus would start a two-year investigation into the Webb City Police Department, one which would put me on the map as a reporter … and start a series of criticisms of my reporting methods that have lasted to this day.

◆ ◆ ◆

The article ran in the Oct. 24, 1990, Carthage Press, under the headline "Tape seems to back up Carterville man's claim." Neil Campbell was a cautious editor, sometimes overcautious, and this story was a prime example. In addition to the word "seems" in the headline, Neil packed one "allegedly" after another in the text of the article, under the mistaken impression that the word serves as protection for any libelous items that happen to slip into a newspaper.

The article started, "An audiocassette recording allegedly made at the Webb City Police Department after the arrest of Vince McCarty Oct. 6 appears to back up the Carterville man's claim that he was brutally beaten by three Webb City officers." The next paragraph nearly drove me crazy, but I couldn't talk Neil out of injecting "allegedly" in a spot where it totally distorted the meaning of the words. "A copy of the tape reportedly has been turned over to the FBI which allegedly is investigating the incidents. The Carthage Press obtained another copy." In other words, my confirmation from an FBI source was not enough to remove allegedly and made it appear as though we were not sure of the FBI's involvement. Unfortunately for me, my FBI source was willing to verify my information, but there was no way he would allow me to use his name. So I had verification from the people who turned the tape over to the FBI and from the FBI, and a step-by-step verification of each portion of the tape to make sure I had the same one the FBI had, but that was not enough. Still, I was the only one who appeared to be disturbed by the safety precautions. The story still had a powerful impact when it hit the streets in Webb City.

The article continued, "The tape indicates that McCarty, who was arrested by Webb City police on a Jasper County bad check warrant, was beaten after he urinated in an interrogation room and refused to mop it up.

"The tape appears to feature McCarty screaming for the policemen to stop beating him and threats from night shift supervisor Lou Angel to teach him not to do that kind of thing in Webb City."

During much of the article, I quoted from the police report submitted by reserve officer Bob Hataway, who did not take part in the beating, and who was deeply disturbed by it. Hataway noted that McCarty made two requests to go to the bathroom. I related what the tape revealed about what happened next. "After another request was made, McCarty can be heard on the tape stating his intention to go ahead and go to the bathroom on the floor."

In his report, Hataway said he told McCarty not to go to the bathroom on the floor and he would find Sgt. Angel and see if McCarty could be taken to the restroom. Hataway could not find Angel and when Hataway returned to the interrogation room, McCarty was urinating. Hataway told Officer Scott Malone what had happened.

On the tape, Malone can be heard telling McCarty, "You're going to clean it up or you're going to have a dent in your head." The next sound was water running, then Malone said, "Clean it up, boy!"

At that point, the sounds of a struggle could be heard. "Don't you f-—with me, you hear me" Malone said. After that, the only sounds that can be heard are McCarty screaming for Malone to stop.

Hataway described the situation in his report. "Officer Malone had the mop bucket and mop in the interrogation room and was trying to make Mr. McCarty take hold of the mop, but he refused. Officer Malone then tried to put a control hold on the prisoner. It involved grabbing hold of the prisoner's two forefingers and applying pressure so as to control the prisoner through pain infliction. It took Officer Malone several attempts, then he finally started escorting Mr. McCarty across the hall to the cell, without resistance." Hataway said that Malone became violent with McCarty when McCarty tried to avoid going into the cell. Malone went to find Sgt. Angel. Hataway said he asked McCarty to stand back so he could lock the cell door and the prisoner offered no resistance. On the tape, McCarty can be heard saying, "He hit me for no reason. He bloodied my nose for no reason. He had no right to hit me in the nose like that."

When Malone and Angel return, Malone can be heard telling Angel a different story. "I got him down and I couldn't handle him by myself. The (expletive deleted) hit me and I didn't do nothing."

Angel said, "It's time we got him out for a little exercise, don't you think?"

Angel and Officer John Dilliner went into the hallway by the cell and began screaming at McCarty. It was difficult to tell which officer shouted the next sentence, but the words were unmistakable. "You've forgotten what's it like to be here in Webb City."

Angel shouted at Hataway to get the cell key; Hataway told him it was in a desk drawer. According to Hataway's report, Angel fetched the key. After the cell was opened, Dilliner repeatedly hit McCarty with his nightstick while Angel shouted at the prisoner and tried to unlock the door, the report said. When Angel and Dilliner finally were able to enter the cell, Angel can be heard saying, "You won't ever forget what it's like to be in Webb City."

Hataway's report said Dilliner left to get his stun gun. When Dilliner returned, Hataway said, the officer used the stun gun on McCarty twice. Later, Jasper County officers picked up McCarty.

"I left the station in disgust around 5 a.m.," Hataway wrote. "Bothered by the incident, I could not sleep at all. After witnessing the heinous acts and abuses of power, I decided I could not trust the police department to handle this affair internally. What I saw looked like a scene out of the movies about law enforcement in the '50s and '60s. This does not happen in modern law enforcement." Hataway's resignation was included with the report.

Hataway's report, and my article, concluded, "I am truly scared for the citizens of Webb City or anyone passing through our city. Anyone caught on the streets after 10 p.m. is not safe with third shift on patrol. Forget the criminal element!

"Beware of the police."

The Carthage Press account included Dilliner's written report which claimed that Hataway was a coward and had not helped him, Malone, or Angel. The tape backed Hataway's version.

◆   ◆   ◆

There was a certain excitement at The Carthage Press when the report broke. It was not often that The Press ran a story of this nature. I could sense that Neil was a little worried that something would go wrong and that the whole story would fall apart on us. And I will be the first to admit, every time I have written an investigative story, I always wonder if there is something I have missed, is there something that would put this whole story in a different light? And worse than that, I always worried about how my stories would affect other people. I did not mind running stories that indicated people had behaved atrociously, but how would those stories affect their families, how would they affect innocent people who had done no harm to anyone? I thought so much about those things, that sometimes I wondered if I was in the wrong business. As it turned out a few years later, my bosses wondered that, too.

We didn't receive any immediate feedback on the Webb City beating story—no indignant protests from Police Chief Emmett McFarland or any of the officers, no word from the mayor, nothing from the FBI. As much as we did not want to hear anything that would disprove our article, we wanted people to at least notice that we had this big story. The response to the article did not come in the usual fashion … mainly because no one in Webb City had read the story. We did not have a sizable circulation in the town to begin with, having only a few subscribers and leaving papers at racks in two or three convenience stores and at a grocery store.

Clyde Phillips, the Press circulation supervisor, told Neil he had received a complaint from a convenience store owner in Webb City that his customers were upset because there were no newspapers. "He said they were calling right and left," mainly because word was out that the truth about Vince McCarty's beating was in The Press. One store owner indicated that the police officers who were named in the article bought all of the papers, and then immediately burned them.

An employee at the Broadway Market told me all of its newspapers had been purchased by one person, but he would not tell me who it was. I called a few minutes later, slightly disguising my voice, had that employee put another one on the line, and the woman, who I had met at a city council meeting, told me that the newspapers were bought by Sgt. Lou Angel.

The next call went to Chief McFarland, "I saw Lou reading *The Carthage Press*," McFarland told me before I was able to explain to him why I was calling. McFarland quickly added to his statement, saying he had no knowledge of Angel buying newspapers and destroying them.

How many of the newspapers reached the reading public, we never knew, but we had no returns from Webb City outlets that day. Every paper was either sold, destroyed, or both.

By this time, Angel, Malone, and Dilliner had been put on desk duty until an internal investigation was completed. No one had expected the investigation to amount to much, and as we quickly discovered we were going to be the only ones pursuing the story. The Joplin Globe by this time had moved Andy Ostmeyer to another beat and his successor did not seem to have much of an interest in the activities of the midnight shift or the plight of Vince McCarty.. The story did not interest the TV stations.

I had a feeling that the beating of Vince McCarty wasn't the real story. Something much bigger was going on in the Webb City Police Department.

Over the next several months, as I continued to cover the story, I began to develop numerous sources in and around the department and around Webb City's municipal government. Those sources included police officers. There were a number of good officers in the Webb City department who were not happy that they were painted with the same brush as the renegades who had beaten McCarty. I was able to get officers and former officers to provide information, verify tips, and to point me in the right direction any time I got off track.

My best sources were three members of the Webb City Council, who were highly displeased with the way Mayor Phil Richardson and their fellow council members were handling the police situation. For a long time, the three council members, all women, would not allow me to use their names, but almost two years later, as the situation reached a crisis point, they went on the record, and that enabled me to use much more information that I had but had been unable to use up to that point.

And, as was usually the case during one of my investigations, much of the information came from documents, some from the courts, some from the city.

When the three officers were questioned by members of the Webb City Personnel Administration board, Sgt. Angel said there was no way he could have beaten McCarty.

"If I had beaten him, he would have looked a lot worse," Angel said.

The three officers' attorney, Mark Elliston, asked, "Could you have maimed McCarty?"

"Yes, I could have. I could have broken his kneecaps. I could have hit him in the Adam's apple. I could have poked his eyes out or smashed his ear drums. Apparently, there's some movements about some moral obligations going around so I purposely avoided any excessive techniques." Yes, he really did talk like that.

After the three officers testified in the hearing, the audiocassette was played, despite Elliston's vigorous objections. The Personnel Administration Board voted unanimously to have Chief McFarland fire the three officers. On Nov. 13, 1990, the council upheld that decision. After the meeting, McFarland said, "My boys were crucified. They were guilty until proven innocent."

Three months after the officers were fired, I confirmed that Angel and Dilliner were still frequent visitors at the police station, stopping by to have coffee and to chat with the chief, and they had never cleared out their lockers. Malone's locker was also filled with his belongings. The three former officers had never turned in their uniforms and Dilliner had been seen in Webb City wearing his city-issued jacket.

All three still had their badges.

After I passed along that information in a page-one Press article, the lockers were cleaned out and the items returned within two days.

Meanwhile, Vince McCarty, encouraged by the FBI investigation into the violation of his civil rights and the authentication of the audiocassette, prepared to sue the city. The insurance company eventually settled with him, reportedly for $30,000. Angel, Dilliner, and Malone also sued the city and despite the fact that he was working for the mayor and the city council, Chief McFarland stood squarely behind the fired officers.

On April 23, 1991, he told me, "I would love to have them back. They're three pretty good officers. They're good officers and we're shorthanded. It's hard for us to do the kind of job we should be doing for the people of Webb City if we don't have the manpower to do it."

In May 1992, Councilwoman Virginia Holder complained to Mayor Richardson about two posters on the front window at the police station advertising Lou Angel's karate studio. "Here is a man who is suing the city and we're advertising his business for him."

McFarland said he had no choice in the matter. "We will put up any sign. All someone has to do is ask. We'll put their ad up on our windows. No one's any better than anyone else. As long as there's nothing derogatory in the ads, I don't see anything wrong in putting them up. He came in and asked if he could put it up. We're not going to treat him any different than anyone else because of the lawsuit."

Besides, McFarland added, "The law doesn't allow me to discriminate against anyone."

◆   ◆   ◆

Between October 1990, and August 1992, The Press ran probably two dozen stories, building on information from nearly a dozen sources I had developed within the city. Many of the best stories came from my interviews with the mayor and Police Chief McFarland.

In late July 1992, I finally hit the jackpot, when city council members turned over a 15-page document entitled "Items for Discussion by the Police, Fire and Ambulance Committee." The report indicated the police department's night shift had harassed minorities and teenagers (minority or not), using racial slurs, and administering beatings that put them in hospital emergency rooms. Other accusations leveled against night shift officers included assault, burglary, contributing to the delinquency of a minor, and a number of civil rights violations.

My investigation showed that McFarland had ignored warnings about his officers, and continued to praise them as "good officers."

According to the report, the following complaints had been received about McFarland's "good officers."

—The beating of a black man

—The beating of a Webb City teenager, who was choked and warned that if he told anyone, the officer would kill him

—Another Webb City teen who had been sent to a convenience store to buy two loaves of bread and two packs of cigarettes for his mother was stopped by an officer for a traffic violation and was beaten.

—Another midnight shift officer pulled a gun on a Webb City teen and held it to his head. When he was called on it, the officer told the boy's parents if any complaints were filed, he would say the boy was carrying a concealed weapon. The boy had a butter knife in the glove compartment of his car.

—Two off-duty midnight shift officers pulled a gun on a man in a bar

—One midnight shift officer was at a party where numerous teens were drinking and a half-nude teenage girl was having alcohol poured over her head.

—One officer broke into a vending machine at a convenience store and took items from it.

It probably should not come as a surprise, but the city council members told me that the biggest concern of city officials as they discussed the allegations was not if they were true, but would the city get sued over them?

Some council members were also concerned that the documents would be given to the police and that McFarland or Angel would cause problems for the complainants. After the meeting, Mayor Richardson collected each copy of the complaints, except one, according to those who attended the meeting, then took them and had them shredded. The remaining copy was locked in a safe at City Hall.

Former police officers told me that the city's Personnel Administration Board had also turned a deaf ear to the complaints.

The Webb City police situation rapidly escalated into what appeared to be a three-way battle between the mayor, the city council, and the police chief. City council members funneled secret documents to me that indicated Chief McFarland was investigated for illegally obtaining machine guns for two of his officers for their private use.

Over a 17-month period, I had approximately two dozen scoops, as the Globe totally ceded the story it originally broke to me. One night at a Webb City Council meeting, as we waited for 6:30 to arrive and the session to begin, a prominent businessman approached the area where I was sitting alongside reporters from the Globe and the *Webb City Sentinel.* He started jokingly giving the Globe reporter a hard time. "The *Carthage Press* is really beating you guys on this police story," he said.

The reporter replied, "We could have had those stories, too, but our editors won't let us do THAT kind of reporting."

Why I didn't say anything, I will never know. A hundred responses popped into my mind after it was too late to make any. The reporter never explained what THAT kind of reporting was. If she was referring to my use of anonymous sources, I really do not know what the Globe's policy on that was at that time or now, but no story during the two years I wrote about the Webb City police situation was written solely on the word of one anonymous source. I always had the story confirmed by at least one other source and usually two, and most often, I had documents to back up what I wrote.

The sniping from the Globe continued over the next few months, as I heard stories that a couple of Globe reporters were saying that I was making most of the information up. No one else had anything on Chief Emmett McFarland buying machine guns for his officers' personal use. No one else had the information The Press had run on the beatings of minorities and teenagers and the problems with the midnight shift.

Though the Webb City police investigation was nothing like what Bob Woodward and Carl Bernstein ran into as they tried to unravel Watergate, I kept remembering what they had written in *All the President's Men* about the reaction from other media when they began writing their Watergate stories. As they continued to file one story after another, other newspapers, for the most part, were not jumping on the bandwagon and some of the Post's editors wondered if the story was really worth all of the trouble. I had written dozens of stories about the Webb City Police Department, and while the Globe and the Sentinel had featured articles about the firing of the three midnight shift officers, the firing of four other officers who were accused of insubordination by the mayor, and their subsequent appeals to the Personnel Administration Board, nothing was being written about the major violations I had unearthed in my investigation.

I was fortunate to have an editor and a publisher who stood 100 percent behind my reporting. Neil Campbell and Jim Farley backed me every step of the way and never once failed to publish any of the articles.

The sniping from some of the people at Jasper County's biggest newspaper grew after it was announced that my Webb City investigation was a finalist in the Associated Press Managing Editors national contest. (It lost to the Waco, Texas coverage of the Branch Davidian massacre.) Though no Globe reporter ever said the words (as far as I am aware), the impression was being given that I was either making up the stories or was being used by some disgruntled council members.

And there was enough of an element of truth in what was being said that my reputation suffered. What was not being mentioned, and should have been, is that many of the biggest stories start with people who are unhappy about the way things are going. Do they have an ax to grind? In many cases, yes. Does that place their stories off limits? It shouldn't. Reporters just have to be careful to make sure their stories are not coated with the same bias that their sources have.

The Press ran a three-part story on Webb City in its Aug. 6-8, 1992 editions, including much new information that I had only uncovered in the three weeks prior to the series. Much of that came from the three council members who resigned to protest what they considered to be the mayor's failure to deal with the police problem. The series sold well in Webb City, but nothing happened because of it, as far as I could tell. Six weeks passed without any developments and because of that, it was much easier for The Press' competitors to say that I had blown the story totally out of proportion.

And then the trial was held for the lawsuit filed by four of the fired police officers and I had an experience not many reporters ever get to have. I watched as one witness after another testified that the information in the stories I had written was completely accurate. And even though The Carthage Press was not mentioned (and did not need to be) the information that had been running in its pages for months was on all three local television stations both nights during the two-day trial and featured prominently in the Joplin Globe on each of the following mornings.

In my article in the Sept. 22, 1992, Press, I wrote, "In his opening statement, Michael Jerde, a Kansas City attorney, said the officers had been called into (Mayor) Richardson's office July 11, 1991, to give information about McFarland … primarily his purchase of machine guns for the private use of two officers." That statement verified the information that had been included in the Aug. 8, 1992, Press.

The article continued, "Jerde said it would have been illegal for the two officers, Lou Angel and Galen Barlow, to have owned the guns. 'It would have been a criminal offense. They wanted them and the chief said I'll buy them for you.'"

But the information included in the trial was not limited to the machine gun purchases. For the first time in any other source besides *The Carthage Press*, readers and viewers found out about "Items for Discussion by the Police, Fire, and Ambulance Committee." The information, a list of complaints, including some of brutality against the midnight shift officers, had been provided to the full City Council and to the Personnel Administration Board, but a full investigation into its contents had been delayed by other, more pressing matters—the beating of Vince McCarty and the police chief's purchase of the machine guns, Jerde said. Every statement made by Jerde, representing officers Larry Stapleton, Jaryl "Joe" Beckett, Mark Wall, and Michael Malone, was backed up by the testimony offered during the two-day trial.

Not surprisingly, I never heard any apologies for all of the aspersions that had been cast on my reporting abilities and on my journalistic ethics. The other representatives of the media acted as if this story had not existed until it was spoken in that Joplin courtroom.

And I didn't care a bit. It wasn't my story when Andy Ostmeyer broke the news of Vince McCarty's beating nearly two years earlier, but it was mine now and there was no doubt about it.

What came of the situation? Though Emmett McFarland remained as police chief for a few more years, the problems in the Webb City Police Department eventually faded away, the department's stature grew and with the appointment of Don Richardson as police chief following McFarland's retirement, the department's operation became crisp and professional.

The three officers who participated in the beating of Vince McCarty, were removed from Webb City, and as far as I can tell, are no longer in law enforcement.

And to this day, I have no idea who taped the beating in the Webb City Jail.

THE DEATH OF NANCY CRUZAN

During the course of my 22 years as a working (paid) journalist, I had the opportunity to work for and with a number of journalism school graduates and I learned a lot from them, but I always felt it was to my advantage that I had never taken a journalism course. Could I have learned something by taking one? Undoubtedly. But I always felt my Missouri Southern State College teaching degree and my life experiences were just as important.

And above all, I always had a key ingredient for anyone who wants to be successful as a reporter … curiosity. When I became managing editor of The Carthage Press in December 1993, I had four University of Missouri School of Journalism graduates working under me. As far as I could tell, none of them had ever taken a course in working with documents, and if they had what they learned had slipped from their memories. The one reporter of the four who did know how to go through records was my lifestyles editor Amy Lamb, and that was because I had taught her when she worked for me as a teenager at the Lamar Democrat from 1987 to 1989.

My knowledge of records began when I returned to the Democrat in November 1982. Barton County had a new circuit clerk at that time, and though he did not have to do so, Jerry Moyer spent a considerable amount of time showing me how to use court files, explaining the meaning of some of the legal terminology, and pointing me in the direction of some fascinating stories. After he got me started, I never stopped. I went from court documents to land transfers to tax liens, and most importantly to The Turner Report, campaign finance documents and lobbyists' reports.

But my knowledge of records was not being used much when I came to The Carthage Press in 1990. I covered meetings, I took photographs at social events, I filled in on sports coverage—I was having a great time, but I missed being involved in courts and politics, and I missed the joys of digging into a story and finding it taking me in completely unexpected directions.

After six months at The Press, as I related in the last chapter, my luck started to turn with the investigation into the Webb City Police Department. Once again, I was burrowing in and uncovering information, and using documents, this time municipal and court documents, to uncover a story.

My return to courtroom coverage, however, involved a bit of luck and, as is so often the case, being in the right place at the right time.

Pat Halvorsen, a chain-smoking, bespectacled woman in her late 30s, who came to the Press from Missouri Southern State College's Communications Department and its award-winning newspaper, *The Chart*, was the city and courts reporter. Normally, she covered everything that came through the Jasper County Courthouse. However, her day off was on Thursday and on one particular Thursday in October 1990, Pat had made plans that she did not want to break, and it gave me the opportunity to cover a story that had grabbed the interest of the nation … the decision on whether Nancy Cruzan of Carterville, who had been in what doctors called "a persistent vegetative state" for more than seven years had the right to die. Her parents, Joe and Joyce Cruzan, went all the way to the United States Supreme Court for permission to disconnect the feeding tubes that were keeping Nancy alive.

It wasn't just the big story aspect and the nationwide coverage that made me eager to cover the hearing. As a Colt League baseball player circa 1970, I had the pleasure of meeting the Cruzan sisters, Nancy and her older sister Christy. They were bright, they were bubbly, and all of the players on my Triway team were quite taken with them. That summer, I was 14 years old, and I loved baseball so much I was able to play on two teams, the 13 and 14 year old Pony League team, and the 15 and 16 year old Colt League team. Before the game, everyone was flirting with the Cruzan sisters, though I will be the first to admit, my best effort, which I was giving, was not very good. The Cruzan sisters were much more attracted to the older boys on the team.

It was a good night for me baseball-wise. Our team won 11-9 and the winning hit was my two-run double, which was not as impressive as it might sound, because it was simply a bloop fly that landed in the Bermuda Triangle between the first baseman, second baseman, and right fielder … and got stuck in a gopher hole. Two runs crossed, and then we held Carterville scoreless in the bottom of the seventh for the win.

We were at Carterville once more that summer and again I talked with the Cruzan sisters, but unfortunately once again, though I was a pretty good hitter on the field, I struck out off the field.

That was the last time I saw Nancy Cruzan.

I doubt that I ever thought about her again until I read in the Joplin Globe about her accident. On Jan. 11, 1983, Nancy had worked the late shift at Schreiber's Cheese Plant in Carthage. She was driving east on Elm Road and was only one mile from her home when the accident occurred. There were no weather conditions that would have explained why she lost control of her car. It ran off the left side of the road, hit some trees and a mailbox, then swerved back across the road and went off the right side, going through a fence, overturning several times and coming to rest on its top. She may have fallen asleep, authorities speculated.

By the time CPR was administered, her brain had already been deprived of oxygen for about 14 minutes. Six minutes is all it takes to cause permanent brain damage. She was left in what doctors called a "persistent vegetative state." The cerebral hemisphere of her brain, which controlled her thinking and her emotions no longer functioned. All she had left were physical reflexes.

Nearly five years into Nancy's existence between life and death, Joe and Joyce Cruzan asked Jasper County Circuit Court Judge Charles Teel if they could remove the feeding tube that was attached to their daughter … the only thing that was keeping Nancy alive. Teel warned that someone could bring charges against them unless they petitioned to have it done legally. The Cruzans filed the motion in Jasper County Circuit Court and that began the long legal battle. Testimony at the circuit court level was provided by people who said that Nancy had indicated she would never want to be kept alive by artificial means. Nancy had worked for a time at the Stapleton Center in Joplin caring for a retarded three-year-old boy who had to be force fed. During a conversation with other workers at the center, Nancy indicated if she were in that situation, she would want to have the plug pulled.

Teel granted permission to have the feeding tubes removed, but the decision was appealed by Missouri Attorney General Bill Webster, who had taken an interest in the case, and it was sent to the Missouri Supreme Court, which overturned Teel's ruling. The Cruzans and their attorney, William Colby of Kansas City, took the case to the United States Supreme Court. It was the first time the Supreme Court had ever considered a right-to-die case.

The Court ruled that a person does have the right to die, but also indicated state courts should hear the evidence and determine if Nancy really had indicated what she would want to happen.

That brought the case full circle and the eyes of the nation were on Carthage, Mo., that day in October 1990.

Knowing the importance of the case, I walked the two blocks from the Press office to the Jasper County Courthouse and arrived 45 minutes before the hearing was scheduled to begin. As I walked onto the square, I quickly realized I had underestimated the interest in the case. Eight TV satellite trucks were stationed on the north side of the square, representing the three Joplin stations, and stations from Springfield and Kansas City. When I saw that, I hurried a bit, thinking I might have a hard time just getting into the courtroom.

As usual, I took the stairs and not the elevator in the courthouse. The Jasper County Courthouse has one of those old fashioned wooden elevators, but that was not the reason for my reluctance. I have severe claustrophobia (I can't even use fast food drive-throughs) and I am extremely uncomfortable in elevators. When I reached the third floor where Judge Teel's courtroom was located, people were milling about through the hallway. At first, I thought those were the ones who did not manage to find a seat, but it turned out most of the people were simply waiting in the hallway. Except for media and Cruzan family members, there were not many others present for the hearing.

When nine o'clock arrived, the session began. Since the hearing was in front of the judge, and no jury was involved, members of the media were allowed to sit in the jury box. At the advanced age of 34, I was starstruck. I was seated in the jury box with a stringer for the New York Times, the Associated Press reporter, the Kansas City Star reporter, a sketch artist for the New York Times, a sketch artist whose affiliation I never did catch, a reporter from the Springfield News-Leader, and other area print and broadcast reporters. Best of all to my way of thinking, I was seated right beside former KODE reporter, then (and still) working at KYTV, Lisa Richardson, and as much as it pains me to admit it since I should have acted as a thorough professional in my representation of The Carthage Press that day, I was flirting to beat the band. Unfortunately, Lisa Richardson was a complete professional. Oh, well.

During the morning, testimony was offered by Nancy Cruzan's father, who said, "By God, I wouldn't be here today if I thought there was any question about what she would want. They've tried to break us, but they're not going to succeed." Under questioning from the family's attorney, William Colby, Joe Cruzan said the long ordeal had a lasting effect on his family. "I don't know what's normal any more. Somewhere along the line I got eight years older; we've lost interest in a lot of things.

Also frustrating for the straight-speaking construction worker was keeping a handle on his emotions as he talked about Nancy's situation. "You can't say what you'd like to say. I feel like we're playing a game. I have to put my best foot forward."

What really bothered Joe Cruzan were the people who piously proclaimed that they knew what Nancy would want and she would not want her feeding tube removed. "The people who make those comments never knew Nancy and they've never taken the time to get to know us."

The morning testimony was gripping and if things had remained the way they were, I would have had exactly the same story as every other reporter in that room. I was in that jury box, thrilled to be with all of those reporters from those major outlets (and Lisa Richardson), but I was seeing things from the same angle as they were, and hearing exactly the same things in exactly the same way. And what was good for those reporters was definitely not the right thing for the only representative of an afternoon newspaper covering the hearing.

The television stations would have the story on the evening news. Our primary competitor, the *Joplin Globe*, would have the story in its morning edition, as would the *Kansas City Star*, *Springfield News-Leader*, *St. Louis Post-Dispatch*, and even the *New York Times*. This was more than a decade before the internet made it possible to post articles about news events moments after they happen. By the time the story was in The Press the next afternoon it would be stale news, and my approach to covering the hearing would guarantee that.

Fortunately, I was saved by lunch. At 11:30 a.m., Judge Teel dismissed the court for lunch, telling everyone the hearing would resume at 1:30 p.m. I hopped back to the Press office, caught up on some of my work and returned to the courthouse 20 minutes early … and found my seat in the jury box had been taken.

No longer was I one of the bigwigs seated with the New York Times, Kansas City Star, St. Louis Post-Dispatch, and Associated Press. And someone else was sitting beside Lisa Richardson … the lucky dog.

It was the best thing that could have happened to me, but at that point I did not realize it. I saw the Globe's reporter Jo Ellis, who later joined me on the Press staff, seated in a corner. I thought about sitting beside her, but then I had a better idea. A few seats were open, two rows behind Joe and Joyce Cruzan and Bill Colby, so I sat directly behind Nancy Cruzan's nieces, her sister Christy White's daughters, Angela and Miranda Yocum. Angela was a sophomore at Webb City High School at that time, and Miranda was a freshman. I would have a different angle on the story.

In retrospect it seems odd to me that I had to learn a lesson I thought I had learned long before ... you can't worry about what the other reporters are doing, you have to get the story your way, in the best way you can.

As testimony resumed, I noticed Miranda had a sketchpad in her lap, so I leaned forward slightly to see her work and I was stunned. What I saw on her pad was just as good as what I had seen in that jury box from the two professionals. She not only had the scene, she had it down to the last minute detail.

Three more witnesses testified that Nancy had indicated to them she would never want to be kept alive through artificial means if she were left incapacitated in an accident. One of the witnesses was Tom Turner, a man for whom she had worked when she lived in Oklahoma City.

The Cruzan family listened attentively as the man began his testimony, clearly answering the questions that were posed to him by Colby and by Carthage attorney Thad McCanse, who had been appointed by the court to represent "Nancy's interests."

Over and over during the day, we had heard about how much Nancy loved her nieces, the two young women who were seated directly in front of me. At the time of Nancy's accident, Angie and Miranda were eight and seven years old respectively. Nancy had always attended their school activities. If there was a ball-game, she was there; if there was a recital, Nancy was in the front row, her face adorned by an ear-to-ear smile as she proudly watched her sister's girls. Nancy had loved those two girls more than she loved anyone else in her life.

As the testimony continued, Nancy's former boss recollected a conversation he had with her, recalling that she had said she wouldn't want to live as a vegetable because "vegetables can't hug their nieces."

After hearing that, Angie, the older niece, began to cry. Miranda's face was also reddening as she put her arm around her sister's shoulder and began patting her on the back, almost playing the role of the older sister.

The two looked at each other and smiled through their tears. Despite the tragedy of the circumstances, it was still wonderful to know how much Aunt Nancy had loved them. By this time, while continuing to write notes about the testimony in the center of my yellow legal pad, I began jotting down observations about Miranda and Angie, but especially the miniature sketch artist Miranda, in the margins. There was no way I was going to beat the morning newspapers and the television stations on the facts of the hearing, but I was going to have a side-bar that no one else would have.

After Turner left the stand and another witness was called, Joe Cruzan abruptly left the courtroom. Assessing the situation, I did not think it was because he was overcome by the testimony because at that moment, it was not that emotional. Therefore, I guessed, he must be headed for the bathroom … so I jumped up and followed him.

Yes, everything you have always heard about reporters is true. We hound people constantly even in their most private moments, and no moment could be more private than this.

My guess was correct. Joe Cruzan stepped into the third floor bathroom and I was only three or four steps behind him. Being a decent sort of person, I allowed him to complete the task at hand before I identified myself and asked Mr. Cruzan if he could take the time to answer just a couple of questions.

I couldn't have blamed him if he had just told me where to go or simply refused. This man had been riding a pressure-cooker wave of media coverage for years, simply for doing what he thought was right, and here was another jerk reporter collaring him in the bathroom, of all places, and asking for an interview … while the hearing that would determine his daughter's fate was being held a few doors down.

Sounding weary, he sighed and said, "Sure, go ahead."

"I've been watching your granddaughter Miranda. She's quite an artist, isn't she?"

For a few seconds, Joe Cruzan said nothing, then a smile crossed his face, the first one I had seen from him that day. "Yeah, she can really draw," he said. "There have been times I've accused her of copying something, but she does it bigger and better than the original." For the next 10 or 15 minutes, I listened as he told one anecdote after another about his granddaughter. Finally, we returned to the courtroom.

Miranda had momentarily put her sketch pad aside as her mother took the stand. Christy White talked about the toll the court battle had taken on her daughters. "At times, they've had to defend our position. Kids will tell them that it's not right, that's not what God would want.

'And everything they're in, a parade, anything at school … I'm kind of like I am right now," she said as tears trickled down her cheek. "Nancy was always there at all the functions the girls participated in. They know when they do something at school, Mom is going to have tears in her eyes." Mrs. White said the girls were more concerned about the effect the ordeal was having on Joe and Joyce Cruzan than they were about themselves. "She loved the girls. Her love for children was so strong."

As the hearing ended, the mini-skirted Miranda hopped out of her seat, sketchpad in hand, walked directly to Bill Colby and gave him the courtroom sketch. "Here's you, how do you like it?" Miranda asked.

"That's good. That's really good."

Colby, who had heard enough emotional testimony during the three years of hearings to build a permanent wall around his heart, was clearly touched by the gesture. "I've never been given one of these before." He thanked Miranda and carefully placed it in his briefcase, pausing to take another long look at the artwork.

I hung around the courtroom until the family left, then bolted for The Press. Writing the story was an interesting experience. Though my deadline was not until the next morning, I wanted to write while it was fresh on my mind, plus I had company in the Press newsroom. Though I was later told I shouldn't have done it, I opened our doors to Terri Gleich, the Jefferson City reporter for the *Springfield News-Leader*, and Lane Beauchamp of the *Kansas City Star*, who needed to write their articles and get them sent to headquarters before deadline.

By this time, however, I was no longer the starstruck reporter of that morning, I was a reporter ... period.

It did not take me long to write the "main" story, the one about the testimony, the one that would already be wrapping fish by the time The Press hit the streets. After that, I worked on the sidebar. I probably did three drafts before I found the tone I was looking for. After that, I kept touching up the story for a couple of hours before I was satisfied.

My job was not yet finished, though. I had some lobbying to do the next morning. I was at the Press office well before my usual 7:30 a.m. arrival time and when Neil Campbell walked in, I was ready with my argument. I wanted to make the sidebar the main story and the main story the sidebar. Neil liked the idea, placing the package at the top of page one with the perfect headline for our feature lead story—"Vegetables can' t hug their nieces," with the subhead "Nancy Cruzan right-to-die case takes a toll on Webb City youngsters."

Now all that was left was to wait for Judge Teel's decision.

Judge Teel took the testimony under consideration and on Dec. 12, 1990, he ordered the feeding tubes removed. In a written statement, Joe Cruzan said, "I suspect hundreds of thousands of people can rest free, knowing that when death beckons they can meet it face to face with dignity, free from the fear of unwanted and useless medical treatment." Two weeks later, Nancy Cruzan, whose life ended on that county road nearly eight years earlier, died.

The end did not come peacefully for the Cruzan family as protesters gathered around the Southwest Missouri Rehabilitation Center in Mount Vernon where Nancy had been a patient for several years. Even though many of the protesters were calling him a murderer, Joe Cruzan still had sympathy for them. He knew they believed in what they were doing, just as he believed in what he was doing. On one particularly cold night, he took them hot coffee because, as he said, "No one should have to be cold."

For a time, Nancy's sister, Christy, ran the Nancy Cruzan Foundation, helping people who faced similar situations. "I think we've come a long way," she told the Associated Press in 1996. "There are a lot of caring medical professionals ready to listen to what patients want. I truly believe ... because of Nan's case ... there are a lot of families that won't have to go to court now."

Missouri went from being behind other states in providing patients the right to control their own destinies to establishing a living will law that makes sure that what the patient wants is taken into consideration. The public awareness created by the Nancy Cruzan case made it easier for people to put into writing what they would want to have done for them medically if they should ever be incapacitated.

Missouri also now has a durable power-of-attorney law, put into effect shortly after Nancy's death that allows a person to name another person who will make the life-and-death decision if it needs to be made. The Cruzan case also made a difference on the federal level. The Federal Patient Self-Determination Act, primarily sponsored by former U. S. Senator John Danforth of Missouri, requires hospital officials to tell patients about their right to determine in advance what should be done and then requires the hospitals to honor those wishes.

Joe Cruzan committed suicide in 1995. His life had never been the same since Nancy's accident. An intensely private person, he suddenly against his will became a celebrity with many sworn enemies who felt he had no right to make a life-and-death decision for his daughter.

Joyce Cruzan died in 1998. The Christmas holidays will always bring bitter-sweet memories for the remaining members of the family. But they do know that their sister's life ... and her death ... made a difference.

Their attorney, Bill Colby, was also greatly affected by the case. He took a leave of absence from his law firm to write a book on the Cruzan case. Earlier, on the fifth anniversary of Nancy's death, he wrote an op-ed article for The Kansas City Star, in which he said what he hoped would be the lasting impact of Nancy Cruzan and the court battle that earned her the right to die.

"The more information we provide while healthy, the more each of us communicates with our loved ones, the greater the chance that we will empower those loved ones to ask the right questions and make the decisions we would choose at the end of life."

In that article, Colby described the call he received from Joe Cruzan the night that Nancy died. "When Joe saw that Nancy was no longer breathing, he reached up and gently closed her eyelids. As we wound up (our) conversation early that morning, I asked Joe, 'What are you going to do now?' He replied, 'Well, I guess we are going to go home.'"

BILL WEBSTER:
THE FALL OF A PRINCE

It's hard to remember that there was a time when people in the know thought Bill Webster had a direct ticket to the White House. Webster, the son of Dick Webster, R-Carthage, possibly the most powerful state senator in Missouri history, had been groomed early for greatness. He rose quickly through the Missouri House of Representatives, then to the position of attorney general, the same platform from which his fellow Republicans, John Danforth and John Ashcroft, had been launched into the national spotlight.

It came as no surprise when the Carthage Senior High School graduate announced his candidacy for governor in 1992. Ashcroft had just finished his second four-year term and it appeared that Webster had an easy road to the governor's mansion.

First, Webster had to get the Republican nomination. At that time, Missouri had four statewide officeholders. In addition to Ashcroft and Webster, Wendell Bailey, a glib, used car salesman with a good-old-boy approach, was state treasurer, and another southwest Missourian, Roy Blunt, was secretary of state. Both men were ambitious and both elected to take their chances at the nomination.

Whoever won would take on the Democratic nominee, either Lieutenant Governor Mel Carnahan or St. Louis Mayor Vince Schoemehl.

I was the political reporter for The Carthage Press at that time and I probably had the most fun I ever had as a reporter covering the ups and downs of the 1992 governor's race.

My part in the coverage did not actually begin until January. At that time, I had been with The Press for close to two years. I had worked for seven and a half years as managing editor of The Lamar Democrat, was 34 years old, and did not see much of a future at a twice-weekly newspaper, so I called Neil Campbell, the managing editor at The Press and asked him if he was still interested in hiring me as a reporter.

Looking back on that conversation, I realize now how much nerve it took to make that call in March 1990. After all, it was 1986 when Campbell and Publisher Jim Farley tried to get me to leave the Democrat and work in Carthage. But I was lucky and Neil said he was still interested and we set up a time to talk about it.

I agreed to come to work at The Press, for the same $250 a week salary I was receiving at Lamar, but with the promise of frequent pay increases if things worked out. At first, I was the area reporter, covering news in Webb City, Sarcoxie, Jasper, Carterville, and all of the small communities that surrounded Carthage. I also served as backup for Carthage coverage and backed up Sports Editor Kevin Keller. For my first two years, I was the jack-of-all-trades at The Press.

At that time, the Press had an eight-person staff, with Campbell, Keller, me, lifestyles editor Nancy Prater, city/courthouse reporter Pat Halvorsen, two long-time mainstays, veteran city editor Jack Harshaw, who had been at Carthage since graduating from the University of Missouri School of Journalism in the early 1950s, veteran reporter and author Marvin L. VanGilder, and staff photographer Catherine Ross.

I had a great time during my first three years at The Press, because all I did was reporting. I did not have the editorial duties that took up so much of my time at Lamar. I covered city council meetings, school board meetings, school activities, and had a chance to do some investigative reporting. No two days were the same, which is one reason why so many people are attracted to journalism.

One day after I had been at the newspaper for nearly two years, Farley called me into his office, and told me I was going to be on the newspaper's Editorial Board. Up to that point, I was unaware we had an editorial board, but I didn't say that. The board's next meeting was scheduled for 1:30 that day in the Press conference room.

After the newspaper was put to bed, I stepped into the conference room. It wasn't the first time I had been in that room. Each night at 6 p.m. if I was still in the building, I turned on the small television set in the corner of the room, and flipped through the channels, seeing if any of the local television stations had landed a story that I had somehow missed. The room had a long table situated directly in the middle and windows all around, through which you could see Carthage Senior High School and the United Methodist Church. Campbell held staff meetings in the conference room 2 p.m. every Tuesday, but this Editorial Board was something different. From the way it had been described to me, this was an extremely important and something I should take as an honor.

I sat down, waiting for the others to arrive, and jotted some notes of things I needed to do after the meeting ended. The others wandered in one by one, we talked about the day's newspaper and waited for Jim Farley to arrive.

Farley, who stood well over six feet tall and was constantly smoking a cigarette, entered the room, checked quickly for an ashtray then took his customary seat at the head of the table.

The Carthage Press Editorial Board consisted of Farley, Campbell, Harshaw, VanGilder, and me. I quickly learned there was only one topic on the agenda—the endorsement of Bill Webster for governor.

Looking back on that day, I don't know why that took me by surprise, but it did. "We're talking about endorsing him for the Republican nomination, aren't we?" I asked.

For some reason, all eyes turned toward Marvin VanGilder at that point. No one said a word and Marvin was looking at me as if I had just uttered some blasphemy. Neil looked a bit nervous. Jim seemed to be enjoying myself. Looking back on that day, I have a feeling he asked me to be on the Editorial Board for just this purpose. Even after nearly two years, I did not know how things worked in the community of Carthage and at *The Carthage Press.*

VanGilder had served numerous stints at The Press, had also been a fixture in local radio with his deep, sonorous voice, and had written several well-received historical books, including "The Story of Barton County," about the county in which he grew up. At this point, it was generally considered that his journalism career was on the downswing. He was already in his 60s and was headed toward retirement. I did not realize just how much it meant to him and to the elite in Carthage to have their own Bill Webster elected to the top post in the state.

VanGilder stared directly at me, then began speaking to me as if I were the child who walked into the visitation and said, "Wow, this place is gloomy. Who died?" "Randy, we are not endorsing Bill Webster for the Republican nomination," Marvin said, carefully enunciating each syllable. "We are endorsing him for governor."

"We don't have any Democrats around here, anyway," Farley said, trying to lighten the mood. (Farley was a Democrat, by the way.)

I did not learn my lesson. "What about Roy Blunt and Wendell Bailey?" I asked. "Shouldn't we look at what they have to offer before we make any endorsement?"

VanGilder explained the situation to me. Bill Webster was from Carthage. Bill Webster could do more for Carthage than any other candidate ... "and we have to be the first newspaper to endorse him for governor."

"Why?" I asked.

"He's from Carthage."

"But he's running for governor of Missouri, not governor of Carthage."

Farley jumped into the conversation. "We're going to endorse Bill Webster," he said.

After that, the conversation centered on what VanGilder would write in the endorsement, which was scheduled to run later that week in The Press. I didn't offer any thoughts.

That was how *The Carthage Press* beat everyone to the punch in endorsing Bill Webster. And newspaper endorsements were a critical part of the 1992 Republican gubernatorial race. Roy Blunt proudly noted that he was supported by nearly every daily newspaper in the state of Missouri.

There were two holdouts who did not endorse the secretary of state, however—the *Joplin Globe* and *The Carthage Press*. But don't put The Press and the Globe on equal terms—we were the only newspaper in the state of Missouri to endorse Bill Webster twice.

A PROUD MOTHER

One of the most irritating things politicians do is to create events. Today, when Missouri Governor Matt Blunt or any other governor signs a bill into law, they don't just do it once, they hold signing ceremonies in several towns, with several pens, with the idea of receiving favorable publicity from several newspapers and several television stations.

And it works every time.

It is also done when politicians announce their candidacy. Logically, you would assume that once someone has announced that is the only time it can be done. You would, of course, be wrong. Nowadays, candidates announce they are forming exploratory committees, then they announce they will announce, followed by a series of announcements.

Oh, how simpler things were in 1992, at least on the state level. I don't recall any of the gubernatorial candidates forming exploratory committees, but *The Carthage Press'* favorite candidate and favorite son, Attorney General Bill Webster, scheduled a series of stops across the state to officially announce his candidacy and he sure took his sweet time about it. After all, The Press had already endorsed him two months earlier. You would think with that kind of support, and with his loving friends and family surrounding him, he would have scheduled an announcement stop in Carthage, but instead he opted for Missouri Southern State College (now Missouri Southern State University) Neil Campbell assigned me to the rally and told me Webster's "people" had already told him there would be no interviews (except we could watch him being interviewed by the local television stations and take notes). So my job was to find something to make The Press' story stand out. That was always my biggest challenge. Since The Carthage Press was, and is, an afternoon newspaper, we always had the story after everyone else had already run it. In this case, the Webster announcement would already be on the 6 and 10 p.m. news on the local TV stations, and our main competition, the *Joplin Globe*, would have an article the next morning. The Press usually did not hit the streets until after two o'clock.

I arrived at Southern about 20 minutes before the rally and immediately began taking notes. I always tried to write down little thoughts about the atmosphere, description of the people, the signs, the crowd, and anything else that might add a bit of color to the story.

Standing front and center in a dark blue dress was a stately woman in her 60s, one whom I immediately recognized. Janet Webster, the widow of Sen. Dick Webster, and mother of the attorney general, was there to see a dream come true. As we waited for her son to arrive, I managed to talk with her for a few moments.

Bill Webster had announced his candidacy in several other venues that day, but this was the only one his mother was going to see. "I'm so proud and I'm so pleased," she said. "His father always took him around when he was at Jefferson City. Bill learned a lot from Dick."

She reflected on her son's successes as he grew up in Carthage. "He was in debate, dramatics, he did some carpentry, photography, he worked at a radio station, he was a disc jockey and a newsman.

"Bill was interested in everything."

Or he couldn't hold a job, I thought, but I wisely kept the comment to myself.

Though Dick Webster died in 1990, he lived long enough to see his son elected to statewide office. "Dick was pleased when Bill became attorney general," Janet Webster said. "He would be very pleased by this. He knew Bill was planning on running."

Trying not to overstay my welcome, I asked only a few more questions, the final answer coming just before Bill Webster and his entourage entered the Connor Ballroom at Billingsly Student Center.

Janet Webster did not approach her son. She quietly took an aisle seat, not even sitting on the front row, but on the second row of blue metal folding chairs. She watched intently as her son, flanked by his wife, Susan, told the packed ballroom how he planned to make changes in the state's education funding, welfare programs, and budget practices. As I jotted down the words Bill Webster said, I kept an eye on his mother, who watched him with adoring eyes. She smiled through his entire speech, even as tears trickled down her face.

When the speech was finished and the applause echoed across the room, Janet Webster quietly took a handkerchief and dabbed it across her face.

I was about to leave, but I decided to go back and talk to Mrs. Webster for a few moments.

"It was quite a moment when he stood up there," she said. "It was sad for me because Dick couldn't be here to see this, but I feel like Dick knows everything that goes on.

"And I know he's pleased."

At that time, no one, except perhaps for Roy Blunt, had any idea that Bill Webster's incredible rise in the political firmament was destined to be accompanied by an equally meteoric collapse.

THE MAN WITH THE PLAN

It did not happen often, but every once in a while a member of an endangered species would cross the borders of Jasper County and make its way into Carthage.

While doing my daily check of my sources, one hinted that an endangered species, a Democrat, might be coming to Carthage. Even though our early and somewhat unwarranted endorsement of Bill Webster's candidacy might suggest otherwise, The Carthage Press under the direction of Neil Campbell was a fair and impartial newspaper. Our editorials might sing the praises of Carthage's own Bill Webster, but if another candidate came into town, we would offer coverage ... it just might not include quite as many pictures or receive as many column inches. So when I told Neil I was going to cover Lieutenant Governor Mel Carnahan's visit to Carthage, he quickly gave me the OK.

It was the evening of March 4, 1992, still early in the campaign, and Carnahan was coming at that time for good reason. No Democrat was ever going to appear in Jasper County after March or April. The county was and is solidly Republican and common practice at that time was to make a cursory stop early in the campaign, never return until after the election ... if then. (That plan was altered successfully in the 2006 U. S. Senate race when State Auditor Claire McCaskill's visits and strong showing in Jasper County and Southwest Missouri helped her eke out a victory over incumbent Jim Talent.)

I parked myself near the doorway of Bob and Faye's Restaurant on the south city limits of Carthage and waited for Carnahan to arrive ... and waited ... and waited. I wasn't in any big hurry to get home so it didn't matter to me when the lieutenant governor arrived, but others were growing a bit more anxious.

As I described it in the March 6, 1992, Carthage Press, "Debbie Hensley's face was a bright crimson as she replaced the pay phone on the hook. Debbie's parents, Betty and Pete Tiller, were in charge of bringing Lieutenant Governor Mel Carnahan to the restaurant where he would speak to members of the Jasper County Democratic Women's Club and other Democrats."

I could make a cheap joke and say there were three people in the room, but that would be far from accurate. In fact, the room was jam packed, leading me to wonder if there were not more Democrats in Jasper County than I had been led to believe … or if someone had imported Democrats from upstate.

At the time, Debbie Hensley was frantically calling her parents' car phone, Mel Carnahan was about 15 to 20 minutes late.

Her first call was a total washout. Mrs. Hensley could hear her parents, but her parents could not hear her. The second call was the one I had described in my article. When the call went through, she said, "Dad," and she was answered by a male voice, and had a brief conversation.

When she got off the phone, she turned, looked at me, her face still a bright red, and said, "I just called the lieutenant governor Dad."

Meanwhile, other Democrats were talking about the evening's activities. One man asked Jasper County Democrat Ruth Ruppert, "Is Clinton coming tonight?" Of course, at that time Bill Clinton was governor of Arkansas and was still considered a long shot for the Democratic presidential nomination.

"No," she answered, "but our next governor is."

"Hearnes?" the man asked, referring to Warren Hearnes, who had been governor during the 1960s.

"No," Mrs. Ruppert politely answered. "I said our next governor, not our ex-governor."

A few moments later, the car pulled into the restaurant parking lot and Mel Carnahan emerged, walking quickly. He slowed down when he entered the restaurant and the Tillers introduced me and he agreed to a quick interview.

At that time, Carnahan had a reputation as a competent, but boring politician. In a state where Webster had an almost rock star presence, Wendell Bailey a folksy, stereotype southern sheriff type of charm, and Roy Blunt a reputation for cool competence, Carnahan fit the late comedian George Gobel's description of himself on a night he was seated with Johnny Carson, Bob Hope, and Dean Martin. Carnahan came off looking like an old pair of brown shoes.

On that night, Mel Carnahan told me he was the "man with a plan."

"There is a mood for a change," he said. "People want someone in the governor's mansion who has an agenda." That was an area in which the current governor, John Ashcroft, had failed miserably, Carnahan said, especially in the areas of jobs and education. "I am not a big government person, but a governor has to set the agenda and marshal the support for it.

"Take jobs. We have a fine Economic Development department, but we haven't got a plan." Carnahan said he had dealt with companies that had been turned down for federal grants because the state had no economic development plan. "The Ashcroft administration has been sort of rudderless, drifting around."

The problem in education was evident, Carnahan said. The lieutenant governor, who had been a school board member for five years, said, "It is very clear that teachers are being called on to do everything except teach. They're loaded down with paperwork, they counsel, they police ... we require teachers to do everything except what we need them to be doing, teaching our children.

"We have to reorganize our priorities in education and if we do, the quality will go up. We have to allow our teachers to return to the classroom." In these days of No Child Left Behind, Mel Carnahan's words still ring true.

Carnahan also made it clear that southwest Missouri was going to be a big part of his campaign. "I have not written off Jasper County or Carthage," he said. "And I won't even if Bill Webster is the Republican candidate."

He continued, "The people in southwest Missouri have always been good to me. I'm determined to be the governor for all of Missouri.

"We're going to be here a lot," Carnahan said, with the general election still eight months away.

It was the last time Carnahan was seen in Jasper County in 1992. I never held that against him, however. His primary opponent, St. Louis Mayor Vince Schoemehl, never came to Carthage at all.

WHERE EVERYBODY KNOWS YOUR NAME

In this day and age when the Internet has revolutionized political reporting, it is hard to remember there was a time when it was difficult to know what our politicians were doing during a statewide campaign.

Today, we can go to the websites of papers throughout the state, the websites of the candidates themselves, and blogs galore with information both favorable and derogatory toward the candidates.

We can Google them and find out what the candidates have said or what others have said about them. Their voting records, campaign contributions, and the records of the gifts they have received from lobbyists are available in moments.

None of that was available in 1992. Sure, you could always work the phones, and that is what I did, and what other political reporters did, but you were always limited in the amount of information you could collect. That was especially true when you worked for a smaller daily newspaper or a weekly.

The Carthage Press still had an eight-person staff in 1992, though some of the personnel had changed. By the time late spring arrived, Randee Kaiser, who had worked for me at the Lamar Democrat, was the sports editor, and another MU graduate Jackie Hosey had replaced Catherine Ross as staff photographer. Glenita Browning, formerly a reporter for the Marshall, Missouri newspaper, was the city/courthouse reporter. Neil Campbell, Jack Harshaw, Marvin VanGilder, Nancy Prater, and I comprised the remainder of the staff.

I did not have an opportunity to do extensive political reporting, due to my other responsibilities. I was still covering a number of area towns, doing more sports than before, writing features, and covering meetings.

Anytime a politician arrived in Carthage, after he met with Jim Farley and Neil Campbell, he was steered in my direction. Then, as now, I kept files on the candidates enabling me to quickly review them before these drop-in interviews. For the most part, that was the full extent of the political coverage, but there were a couple of notable exceptions.

One was when I told Neil Campbell I would have the results of the Garrison Avenue Poll for the next day's page one. Neil was pretty excited about it. He could not believe that I had the initiative to commission a poll to add to the newspaper's political coverage. His attitude changed when he found out what the Garrison Avenue Poll was.

I hopped in the red Olds Cutlass Supreme I was driving at the time, drove down Garrison Avenue with a yellow legal pad beside me on the front seat, and jotted down which candidate was named on each sign.

I then wrote an article describing which candidates displayed the best "sign language," and turned it in. Somehow, Neil let me get away with that, and I repeated the stunt several times over the next seven years, eventually even adding a Grand Avenue Poll, so Carthage's other leading street would not feel left out.

My other contribution to allegedly innovative political coverage in 1992 came when I pulled an old National Enquirer trick and dug photos of the gubernatorial candidates, Webster, Blunt, Bailey, Carnahan, and Schoemehl, out of our files, and then looked into the Associated Press photo box and found a photo of actress Rhea Perlman, who played Carla the barmaid on the comedy *Cheers*, which at that time was comfortably situated in the Nielsen Top 10.

Armed with the photos, I did something I always hated—a man-on-the-street interview. I walked the two blocks to the Carthage square, and started approaching total strangers, asking which of the folks in the photos they could identify.

Neil was not happy with the results of my survey, but he ran them on an inside page in the June 29, 1992, Press. I thoroughly expected either Carthage native Bill Webster or Rhea Perlman to win the poll.

As I wrote in that article, "Bill Webster probably won't lose any sleep over it, but a *Carthage Press* random poll (with a 99.9 percent probability of error) shows that 80 percent of the voters don't know who he is."

But it was not the Cheers barmaid who won the poll, but Secretary of State Roy Blunt, with Rhea Perlman finishing second, and our own Bill Webster taking third, among 10 randomly selected Carthage shoppers. No one recognized all six of the photos. Even the winner, Blunt, was only recognized by four out of 10. One young woman said of Bill Webster, "He looks like a judge," following her comment by adding, "and I know a lot about judges." Why I didn't follow up on that statement, I will never know.

My favorite was the woman who immediately recognized Wendell Bailey's photos. "I know Bill Clinton when I see him," she said.

For some reason, that innovative idea also failed to revolutionize the art of political reporting.

EVENTS LEADING UP TO
THE LINCOLN LADIES
SOCIAL

As the area reporter for *The Carthage Press*, one of the communities I covered was Lamar, approximately 25 miles north. Of course, it was a community with which I was familiar and loved a great deal.

I first came to Lamar in March 1978 to interview for a reporting position on the *Lamar Democrat*, which was a daily newspaper at that time. I had not done well in my first newspaper job as both editor and advertising salesman for the *Newton County News* and I was not really sure about my college education. I had attended Missouri Southern for four years, but still needed another year to get my degree and I really wanted to see if reporting was going to be something I wanted to do full time.

I made it clear to the Democrat's editor, Lou Nell Clark, that I would not be able to take the reporting position because I still had two months to go before the spring semester ended, but I wanted a chance to go through the interview and find out about the Democrat.

I have never figured out what it was that Lou Nell saw in me, but two months after that interview, I became the Democrat's sports editor. I only held that position for eight months, before I became a victim of Boone Newspapers' budget cuts, but I already had a warm affection for the community.

It was the Lamar Tigers' head football coach Chuck Blaney, now the principal at Neosho High School, who encouraged me to go back to school and get my teaching degree when my job ended in December 1978.

I did not do so immediately. I planned to return to college in the fall 1979 semester, but a month later, Democrat Publisher Dennis Garrison called me to ask if I would be interested in being the editor of Boone Newspapers' weekly, the *Lockwood Luminary-Golden City Herald*, and I agreed to take the position, for the princely sum of $180 a week, or $50 a week more than I had been making at the Democrat.

That job lasted 10 months until the newspaper went out of business. I worked for Editor Emery Styron at the *Newton County News* from the summer of 1980, starting as a telemarketer, then moving to reporting, and then when Emery left the newspaper, I once again became editor and advertising manager. I did much better at the reporting and editing, but I was still a lousy ad salesperson and in February 1982, that job came to an end.

While I was working at the *Newton County News*, I returned to MSSC, finished my final year of college, completed my student teaching at Diamond Junior High School, and began looking for my first teaching job.

My college advisor never told me that social studies teachers who were not coaches had two strikes against them when it came to getting hired for teaching positions, especially in smaller schools. I only landed a couple of interviews and no jobs. In the fall of 1982, I worked as a substitute teacher in the Diamond and Pierce City school systems, and that experience gave me an incredible amount of respect for people who handle that job. I hated it and I always felt like I was three steps behind the students.

Finally, in November 1982, out of the blue I received a call from Doug Davis, who had been publisher of the *Lamar Democrat* since February 1981. Davis asked me to come in to interview for the editor's job at the Democrat, I landed the position and stayed there for the next seven and a half years.

When I left the Democrat to work at Carthage, I thought I was leaving Lamar behind, but a few months after I started, the city was added to the list of towns I covered.

I was making my rounds during the early afternoon on July 28, 1992. The primary was one week away and I spotted Secretary of State Roy Blunt heading into the studios of Lamar's new radio station KHST (the HST stands for Harry S Truman, Lamar's most famous native son).

Blunt had become persona non grata in Carthage, due to a series of ads in which the secretary of state relentlessly attacked Bill Webster. The ads had helped Blunt narrow the margin and Webster's once seemingly insurmountable lead appeared to be in danger. The ad was one of the best attack ads Missouri politics has ever seen. It showed a carousel and gave the implication, later proven to be true, that Webster was shaking down lawyers for campaign contributions.

I heard it said around Carthage, "Roy Blunt is going to pay for telling those lies about Bill Webster. When Bill's elected governor, Roy Blunt is going to be out of politics," or words to that effect.

But on that day in Lamar, Roy Blunt and his family were making the rounds, and had already been at the Democrat office. Roy was accompanied by his wife (at the time) Rosann, daughter Amy (now a registered federal lobbyist and a law-yer with the powerful Lathrop & Gage firm), and his fresh faced son Matt, barely in his 20s at that point.

Knowing that the biggest event in Republican politics, the Lincoln Ladies Ice Cream Social, was scheduled for that night at Memorial Hall in Carthage, I asked Blunt if he would be attending. "Are you going to go into the Tiger's den?" I said, a bad reference to Carthage's school nickname.

Blunt shook his head. "I don't think so. I don't think it would help me much to be there." He excused himself as the radio station's news director stepped out of his office. I waited with the Blunt family. Amy Blunt, a striking blonde, was talking with a radio station employee and young Matt was standing off to the side, looking out the window, and shifting from one foot to the other as he waited for his father to emerge from the studio.

I had a conversation with Rosann Blunt about everything from the campaign to the weather. She was one of Roy Blunt's biggest assets on the campaign trail. It surprised me to see the studio door open and see the secretary of state headed directly toward me. "You know, Randy, I think I will go into the tiger's den tonight."

I was beginning to look forward to the ice cream social. This campaign was starting to be fun.

THE LINCOLN LADIES ICE CREAM SOCIAL

Every election year, Carthage's top Republican group, the Lincoln Ladies, holds an ice cream social at Memorial Hall and it is an event that I have continued to attend even after my departure from the newspaper business.

There are a number of reasons for that. One, of course, I love politics. Two, I always enjoy renewing my acquaintance with the event's timekeeper, the lovely Mary Lou Teel (formerly Newman) who worked for me for a short while at the Lamar Democrat after she graduated from Jasper High School.

But equally important (and just as sweet as Mary Lou) is the ice cream. The Lincoln Ladies hand out these little containers of vanilla ice cream and I usually am able to sneak two or three while the politicians are working the crowd.

I walked the three blocks from the Press office to Memorial Hall and, as usual, began taking notes on the surroundings. Candidates had arrived hours before the social, putting up their posters and signs, and strategically placing campaign literature on the tables. The setup was the same as it had been for years. The candidates, after shaking hands with the crowd for about an hour, would stroll up to the stage, have a seat on a folding chair and await their turn.

Each candidate was allotted a maximum three minutes to get his or her message across and it was not like these debates on television where the candidate continues to speak after time runs out. After three minutes at the Lincoln Ladies Ice Cream Social, the bell rang and you stopped. Candidates dared not continue, lest some fate far worse than death should befall them.

I could already sense that this Lincoln Ladies social was far different from the norm. I spotted hundreds and hundreds of red, white, and blue balloons tied in the balcony and saw dozens of men and women wearing Webster T-shirts. Several ladies appearing to be in their late 20s or early 30s were wearing red, white, and blue outfits, complete with white mini-skirts, which would have been far more suitable for teenagers than adults. (I wasn't complaining, mind you.)

As the candidate began to meander toward the stage, I still had not seen any of the three GOP candidates for governor. People kept looking at the door, waiting for native son Bill Webster to make his triumphant appearance.

My camera was at the ready. (If you worked for The Carthage Press and came back from a political event without a photo of Bill Webster, you might as well forget about returning to the office and head straight to the unemployment line.) Finally, the door opened and a candidate for governor stepped in.

It wasn't the right one.

"What's he doing here?" a woman sitting a few feet from me asked, tapping the shoulder of a young blond woman standing in front of her when Roy Blunt walked into the room. It wasn't a suit and tie, button-down candidate who came to the ice cream social. Blunt was wearing a long-sleeved shirt and dark slacks, but no suit jacket, and looked more like someone on a Sunday stroll than a candidate for the most powerful position in Missouri state government. I glanced at the woman who asked the question. Naturally, she was wearing a Webster t-shirt and carrying a Bill Webster for Governor sign. I had spotted her handing out Webster campaign fliers earlier.

The young woman responded, "Who?" clearly not having seen Blunt yet. As the woman pointed toward the door, the blonde's mouth dropped open, but she quickly collected herself. "Well, I'll say one thing for him.

"He's got guts."

Blunt worked the outer perimeter of the room, shaking hands, though no one seemed to be overjoyed at his presence. He quickly made his way to the stage and took a seat beside the other candidates.

Future Governor Matt Blunt was not at Memorial Hall that night, but three others whose names are still synonymous with the Missouri Republican Party were. As Bill Webster's mother, Janet, sang a medley of patriotic songs at the beginning of the program, those sitting on the stage, respectfully listening, in addition to Roy Blunt, were attorney general candidate David Steelman, (whose wife Sarah is now state treasurer), and secretary of state candidate John Hancock, now a top GOP operative and blogger for *Missouri Pulse*).

The program began with candidates for Jasper County office and state representative. Situated near the south door, I heard a loud noise coming from outside. I slipped out the door and saw a helicopter landing in the parking lot next door in front of O'Reilly Automotive. A crowd began to gather and watched as Bill Webster stepped off the copter. But the attorney general made no move toward Memorial Hall. He was not going to put himself on the same level with the other GOP candidates.

I slipped through the crowd and asked Webster if he had time for a short interview. He nodded, though I noted at the time, that he did not look me in the eye as he did so. Bill Webster was one of those politicians I always hated to interview. He was always on message. If his message for the day was "We must cut taxes," and you asked him, "Who do you think will win the World Series this year?" he would answer, "We must cut taxes," and not even make a pretense of answering the question.

It wasn't much of an interview. I don't recall how much, if any, of it made the pages of *The Carthage Press*. After a few brief questions and long, but unrelated answers, I thanked the attorney general and returned to the room. I was torn between the need to head toward the front of the room and snap a few photos of the politicians or my desire to head to the back of the room. The siren call of the vanilla ice cream won out, and I had some more to tide me over, before resuming my reporting.

By this time, candidates for statewide office were talking. First were the candidates for attorney general and secretary of state. Then I was surprised to learn there was yet a fourth candidate for governor. Rev. Dwight Watts, Joplin, head of Soul's Harbor, a group which offers shelter to the poor, was the first candidate for governor to speak.

"I have three great loves," he said, "the state of Missouri, Jasper County, and Joplin." Now that's something to say in Carthage, I thought. Watts said he wanted Missouri's government to return to the basics. "Basics is Jesus Christ. All problems can be solved by Jesus Christ."

Just try to tell that to Roy Blunt, I thought. In a room with more than 200 people, nearly all of them angry at him for his series of ads ripping their own Bill Webster, Blunt had to say something that would make it worth his side trip.

After Watts finished, and Blunt was introduced, he patted the shoulder of attorney general candidate John Hall, who was sitting next to him, half smiled and said, "Here we go."

A hush fell over the room as Blunt approached the lectern. You couldn't have blamed him for thinking if that coward Wendell Bailey had shown up, at least he would have another three minutes to think of something to say.

Blunt smiled at the audience. No one smiled back. Blunt couldn't have this crowd angrier if he said, "I don't think there's a one of you who shouldn't be paying more taxes."

I was halfway rooting for him to win the crowd over with the greatest three-minute speech of all time, then he started talking about newspaper endorsements. "Out of 24 newspapers that have endorsed candidates for governor in recent weeks," Blunt said, "22 have supported my candidacy, one supported State Treasurer Wendell Bailey, and the other one divided their endorsement between Wendell Bailey and me."

"No, no," I wanted to shout. "We endorsed Bill Webster twice." I thought if I didn't say it, surely Marvin VanGilder would since he was sitting at a table at about the center of the room. But no one said a word. That damnable lie had been entered into the public discourse.

As you might expect, the Carthage crowd really didn't care which newspapers had endorsed Blunt, or for that matter if any had endorsed him. Blunt's feeble attempt at humor also fell short. He noted that he, Bill Webster and Wendell Bailey had just been at a dinner in Aurora. Bailey opted not to come to Carthage, Blunt said, but he thanked Webster for his kindness. "He offered to give me a lift, but he said I would have to ride on the propeller." It wasn't that bad of a line, but no one laughed.

Blunt did receive a light smatter of applause when he finished his three minutes by promising to work for Republican candidates in the general election, regardless of the primary's outcome.

As he left Memorial Hall, there was an audible sigh of relief. Now that Roy Blunt was gone, it was time to get down to business.

And that's when the lights went off.

The strains of "Born in the USA" by Bruce Springsteen blared across the room. Everyone stood and the balloons were released from the balcony, floating through the air in every direction. Bill Webster entered through the south doorway, a spotlight focused on him every inch of his trip. He began removing his blue suit jacket and as he walked down the aisle toward the stage, he tossed it into the audience. (One of his staff workers caught it.)

Webster made no effort to begin his speech. He stood at the front of Memorial Hall and basked in the adoration of his hometown. Those ladies in the 20s and 30s in their short, red, white, and blue cheerleader-type skirts were jumping up and down.

By this time, I had already been a reporter for more than 15 years, but I was still caught up in the excitement of the moment. No wonder we endorsed this guy twice. He's a superstar.

And so he would have remained if he had just kept his mouth shut. Unfortunately, there was no way any speech Bill Webster could give was going to live up to that kind of introduction.

For the first time, the Lincoln Ladies broke their rule and allowed a candidate to go over the three minute limit. That was another mistake.

It wasn't a bad speech that Bill Webster made that night. It was a routine political speech, no better, no worse than any other the attorney general had ever made. And that night called for something special.

Still as I noted in the July 29, 1992, Press, Webster probably could have recited the Carthage phone book and the audience would have given him a standing ovation.

Webster started with criticism of Federal Judge Russell Clark's desegregation rulings which pumped state money into the Kansas City and St. Louis school districts at the expense of the rest of the state. "Missouri taxpayers are paying for Kansas City students to travel across the nation playing tennis. They're taking Russian fencing lessons, while schools from the rest of the state, including this area, have to struggle to provide students with their basic educational needs."

Webster cited his accomplishments, saying he had made Missouri the state with the highest criminal conviction rate in the United States and had established a consumer aid program which was responding to 60,000 calls a year.

He then turned his focus toward the general election. "I need a big turnout from Jasper and Newton counties, not just now, but in November," Webster said.

Already past the three minutes, Webster launched into an attack on both of his possible Democratic opponents, already putting Roy Blunt, Wendell Bailey (and even Rev. Dwight Watts) in his rearview mirror. Webster blasted Mel Carnahan's call for a $200 million tax increase for education. "That's not what this state needs to attract jobs."

As much as Webster criticized Carnahan, he was even more dismissive of St. Louis Mayor Vince Schoemehl. "He says he wants to do for this state what he has done for St. Louis. This state can't afford that. St. Louis has lost 25 percent of its population and has the highest crime rate in the state.

"We don't want Vince Schoemehl to do for Missouri what he has done for St. Louis.

Webster concluded with commentary on Roy Blunt's remarks about all of the newspapers that had endorsed the secretary of state's candidacy. "It's not my job to do what the editorial boards of the Kansas City and St. Louis papers want. The people I answer to are the state of Missouri."

I waited for Webster to add. "I have received the only two endorsements that matter, and both of them came from The Carthage Press." Those words never came.

Maybe if we had endorsed him a third time.

ELECTION WATCH

A few days after the Lincoln Ladies Ice Cream Social, Neil Campbell stopped me as I headed into the news room and handed me a small slip of paper with the initials "T. F." followed by a phone number and the words "Capitol Plaza Hotel."

It seemed highly unlikely that my editor was trying to set me up with someone and the number indicated whoever T. F. was, this person was in a different area code, so I knew something must be up.

"What's this?"

"Tony Feather called and said you could reach him election night at the Capital Plaza to get a quote from Bill Webster at his election watch party." Tony Feather, a native of Sarcoxie, ran Bill Webster's campaign. Feather is still in the business today, working in 2007 on former Massachusetts Governor Mitt Romney's presidential bid.

Marvin VanGilder, who had the desk next to Neil's added how important it was for Bill Webster's hometown newspaper to have a quote from him in the next day's edition. I agreed. I placed the number in my wallet to make sure I did not lose it, then sat down at my desk in the center of the newsroom and zipped through my messages. Then a thought hit me. I shouted, "Neil, why don't I just go to Jefferson City next Tuesday?"

There was a brief silence, then Neil said, "I like that. I like that. Let me check with Jim."

Moments later, I had my approval for a trip to Bill Webster's victory party. The luster of the Webster campaign had diminished across the state thanks to Roy Blunt's steady bombardment of negative advertising, but Webster still had a comfortable lead in the polls as the campaign reached its final days.

There appeared no doubt that Bill Webster would be the Republican candidate for governor and would most likely face Mel Carnahan in the general election. I was going to witness a slice of Missouri history firsthand. Neil Campbell knew me well enough to know there was a problem with my scenario.

He hesitated, then broached the subject. "Randy, are you sure you can find the Capital Plaza Hotel?"

I thought I heard a few chuckles from all corners of the newsroom, but I ignored them. I had a well-earned reputation for not being able to find anything and I never had been able to make my way anywhere at night. When I first worked at The *Lamar Democrat*, any time my editor, Lou Nell Clark, sent me to cover a fire, bets were taken on how long it would take for me to return to the Democrat office and either ask for directions or simply say I couldn't find the fire.

When I was at Lamar in 1978, I was offended when someone mentioned this weakness. By 1992, I had come to accept it and try to find ways to conquer the problem. "I will make sure I know how to get there," I replied. Neil nodded and seemed to trust my assurances, but elsewhere in the newsroom, I detected skepticism.

That night, I called an old friend of mine, Yvonne Haile, who worked for the State Tax Commission, and asked if she would be willing to go with me to the Webster victory party.

Yvonne, who was from Lamar and whom I had met when she was working in the Barton County Equalization Office, knew me too well. "You not sure you can find your way there?"

I tried to remain calm. "That has nothing to do with it."

She laughed.

"All right. All right. I need some help."

Yvonne, who has since moved back to Lamar, agreed to go. She had been involved in Republican Party activities in Barton County and had an interest in seeing what one of these election night celebrations was like.

I thanked her, we talked some more and as the conversation was about to end, she said, "Are you sure there's not something else you'd like to ask me?'

I couldn't think of anything.

She reminded me I had never been to her home in Eldon, Missouri. "Do you need some directions?"

I sheepishly admitted I did. She started to give them to me and could quickly tell I did not understand her at all, so we agreed to meet at a restaurant right by the Eldon exit.

Everything was set. Now the only thing to worry about was whether Roy Blunt would overtake Webster in the last few days. If he did, instead of a celebration, I would be covering a wake ... and it would be even worse when I got back to the Press newsroom.

◆   ◆   ◆

I left during the early afternoon Tuesday, Aug. 4, for Jefferson City, excited about the prospect of covering a major political story. Just before I left, I broached the possibility of swinging by Roy Blunt's headquarters for a few moments and snapping some photos and getting a few quotes, but that idea was quickly shot down. First, Bill Webster was the candidate from Carthage and second, and even I agreed with this one, there was no guarantee I would ever be able to find Blunt headquarters, and even if I did, I might not find my way back to the Capital Plaza Hotel.

I met Yvonne and her husband, Bobby, at the restaurant, where we had dinner. Yvonne said she would drive, so we took my car back to her house, and her teenaged daughter Rachael decided to accompany us.

I was surprised by how elaborate the victory party was. At first, I thought I was woefully underdressed. Though I was wearing a tie, the first few men I saw were in suits, but as I glanced about the cavernous room, I could see that formal wear was optional. No one had on blue jeans, but many were milling about the room sans ties.

A band was playing up tempo dance music and nearly every other person in the room was taking advantage of the abundant alcoholic drinks that were being served. An entire bank of television cameras was set up in one corner of the room, with stations from Jefferson City, Columbia, Kansas City, St. Louis, and Springfield represented. I had only been there for a few short moments when Tony Feather spotted me and headed in my direction.

He shook my hand, told me how glad he was that The Press had decided to send someone to Jeff City and that the attorney general would be happy to have a one-on-one interview with me. I thanked him. That was to be the first of many times I would be talking with him that night.

Except for Tony Feather, I saw almost no one that I knew, except for Kaare Gjeruldsen from Sarcoxie. I spoke to him for a few moments, talked to Yvonne for a while, but most of the time, I was taking pictures and notes.

Televisions were on in one area of the room and some gathered around them to keep up with the latest election results. It was becoming apparent that it was going to be a celebration. Roy Blunt had narrowed the gap, but Bill Webster was going to be the Republican nominee.

After about an hour, I received my second visit from Tony Feather. This time, he let me know that I might only get a few minutes with Webster. I told him I understood how valuable Webster's time was and I would appreciate any time I could get.

Webster, of course, was nowhere in sight. He would wait until he received the concession call from Blunt. It was going to be a long wait.

As the wait continued, and the dance music continued to play in the background, I began thinking of backup stories and sidebars I could write. I had to come back with enough material to show Neil Campbell and Jim Farley that the trip was a good idea and then maybe they could go along with me the next time I had a bright idea.

When Tony Feather returned, once more without Webster, I knew it was not going to be good news. "Randy, we're not going to be able to let you have a one-on-one. You're going to have to do the interview with the other print reporters."

I tried to impress upon him that I was the only one from his candidate's hometown newspaper. He acknowledged the point, but said there was nothing he could do about it.

After 10 p.m., Bill Webster and his wife, Susan, finally emerged, to a thunderous round of applause. I slipped in close enough that I could hear they were waiting for Roy Blunt to concede … and they were angry that they had not heard from him.

The voices were kept low for a while, and I could not pick up on what they were saying but when Tony Feather headed toward me, I already knew what he was going to say.

"Randy, we're not going to be able to get your interview." He apologized and I have always sincerely believed he was trying to do his best to get me a one-on-one with Webster. Now I had to scramble.

Webster briefly addressed the audience, unable to say much because Roy Blunt had still not conceded the race. "I want to thank Team Missouri (the modest name Webster gave to his campaign) for raising the most money any Missouri gubernatorial candidate has ever had. The bad news is we have to raise more money." That was the closest thing the attorney general's supporters were going to get to a claim of victory during that brief address, so a thunderous round of applause ripped through the crowd.

After he spoke, Webster walked directly to a television reporter and began talking until he caught the high sign being given by one of his campaign workers. "Excuse me," Webster said, abruptly leaving the reporter's side and heading toward a television in the corner of the room. "Roy's on. I want to hear what he has to say."

The band stopped playing and the crowd gathered around the television set, waiting to hear the concession speech that would cement their candidate's victory. But the words that came from Roy Blunt's mouth, though not optimistic, were not an out-and-out concession. Still, some of those surrounding the attorney general saw it that way. "I think that was a concession speech," one said, with another responding, "It was sort of a concession speech. He didn't say he was conceding the election, but he said there weren't enough votes left for him to win."

Webster, his wife Susan, and two of their sons, retired to an adjacent room to wait a short while longer.

About 10 minutes later, a phone rang, Webster was called back into the room, and the phone was handed to Webster. I could hear people speaking in low tones and nearly all of them were saying the same thing. "It's Roy." I snapped a photo of Webster taking the call from Roy Blunt. A leather-lunged Webster supporter, paraphrasing the first President Bush, shouted, "Read my lips, no more Blunt." Webster held a hand over one ear, as he talked into the phone. I wasn't close enough to hear what was being said, but the OK sign that Webster made, followed by the sound of steady applause put the message across. And for the first time all evening, Webster's face featured an ear-to-ear smile.

I was still holding out hope of at least collaring Webster and getting in a question or two. Those hopes were dashed when the television circus began. Webster's media coordinator Renee Howell guided Webster toward the long bank of television cameras, and I watched as Webster, who did not have even one second to spare for a print reporter from his hometown, or any other print reporter, gave a full interview to every television reporter in the room.

One female reporter from a Columbia station had taken her shoes off and for some reason stood on a chair to conduct her interview. I watched in disbelief as the man who appeared on his way to becoming the next governor of Missouri climbed up on the chair beside hers and the interview began.

Deciding that this wasn't going to get me anywhere, I did the same thing I did when Webster had announced his candidacy at Missouri Southern. I was going to tell his story as it was being seen through someone else's eyes and that someone was going to be Susan Webster.

She was talking to another woman when I gingerly approached her and asked her if I could have a brief interview. She agreed and I began asking the basic questions about how the night had gone and how she was feeling. It was your basic typical interview and I needed something better than that, so I asked, "How did you feel when you saw those ads Roy Blunt was running and the things he was saying about your husband?"

At first, I thought she might end the interview right there, but apparently, it was a question she wanted to answer and now that Roy Blunt was no longer a factor, she could get it out of her system.

"Every time one of those commercials came on, I'd tell them, 'It's just politics,'" but she quickly conceded the family had been hurt by the continuous attacks. Now the election was over. "It's a relief, but now we have to start all over again." That didn't seem to be a prospect she was eagerly anticipating.

I had my story, but the night was not over. I watched as Webster continued to run the gauntlet with the remaining TV reporters. When he was done, he and successful attorney general candidate David Steelman stepped forward, the crowd quieted and the two gave the victory handshake that I captured on film and would run on page one of the next day's Press. It was Webster and Steelman standing a few feet apart, shaking hands, while a beaming Susan Webster stood between them. And the entire scene was captured in front of a red, white, and blue "Bill Webster for Governor" sign. Of course, that didn't do me much good since I was shooting my photos with black and white film.

Webster thanked his supporters, made the requisite gracious comments about his opponents, Blunt and Wendell Bailey, and launched a brief attack on the Democratic winner Mel Carnahan.

"I would like to debate Mel Carnahan every day between now and November," Webster said. He blasted what he termed Carnahan's "tax-and-spend philosophy" and said he, Roy Blunt, and Wendell Bailey had one thing in common. "We don't want Mel Carnahan as the next governor." Webster blasted Carnahan's education plan. "This is the first time I've seen in years someone who said from the get-go, 'I think we need to dramatically raise taxes." The attorney general predicted it would be a tough campaign, "one that will be built on issues, ideas, and values." In a reference to Roy Blunt's campaign attacks, without mentioning the secretary of state by name, Webster said, "This campaign wasn't about television commercials and radio. This was about the thousands of people who went door-to-door campaigning for what they believed in."

Webster added, "This is just the first act of a two-act performance. Susan and I invite you back in November for act two."

Webster paid tribute to a person who was not at the Capital Plaza Hotel, but whose presence was deeply felt, "a fellow who was a senator from southwest Missouri," Webster said, referring to his late father. The mention drew a thunderous ovation. The attorney general credited his father, Dick Webster, and his mother, Janet Webster, with teaching him about "family, faith, and friends."

As Bill Webster left, he encouraged everyone to continue to party. With that, Webster, his wife, Steelman and his wife, and Feather all quickly headed toward an exit. If they reached it, my last chance for an interview was gone. How could I return to Carthage and tell Neil Campbell and Jim Farley that their reporter at Bill Webster's victory party had not even managed to ask the winning candidate one question.

Seeing an angle that would enable me to get to the door before the Webster entourage I bolted for the door and got there just before Webster. "Attorney General Webster," I said, "Randy Turner with The Carthage Press. Can I ask you a couple of questions. For one brief moment, I thought he was going to turn me down, but he took a deep breath and said, "Sure, how can I help you?"

I don't know about the others in Webster's group, but I caught a glimpse of Tony Feather's face and I thought he was trying to suppress a smile. I don't believe he had liked having to tell me I wasn't going to interview the candidate.

I knew our Press brain trust, Neil, Jim, and Marvin VanGilder, would want questions related directly to Carthage and Jasper County, so those were the questions I asked, since Webster was not going to stand still for a long interview.

Webster told me he was grateful for the support he had received from Jasper County. "We started this campaign in Jasper County a year ago and I said all along that we would have to have a good turnout there to win. That kind of support turned out to be the difference."

I asked about the general election campaign. Webster said his top priority at the beginning of the campaign would be to put the party together again after the divisive primary. "We will begin to work on that immediately. During our telephone conversation, Roy Blunt made a pledge to me that he will work with me to do that. We had a situation where we had three state officials running for the nomination. Wendell Bailey has been a fine state treasurer. Roy Blunt has been a fine secretary of state. We've had our disagreements during this campaign, but we agree on one thing. We don't want Mel Carnahan to be our next governor."

After the interview, I took stock of what I had. Besides the interview, I had copious notes from the speech, everything that had led up to the speech, the Susan Webster interview, and observations galore. Plus pictures. It was time to go home.

After Yvonne, her daughter, and I reached her home, I said good night, climbed into my car and began the long trek to Carthage. I pulled into the city limits shortly after 5 a.m., turned in my film, wrote my stories, went downstairs and grabbed a nap on the sofa in the lounge. It wasn't comfortable, but I wanted to be there after the film was developed to write the cutlines.

When the next day's Press hit the stands, the headline, which appeared to be about 84 point, read simply "It's Bill." In Carthage, that was all you had to say.

It was the biggest night of the Carthage native's political career ... and it was the beginning of the end.

GENERAL ELECTION

My role in the coverage of the election of 1992 shrunk rapidly after the primary. As noted earlier, the Democratic nominee, Lieutenant Governor Mel Carnahan, never came to Carthage, nor do I remember him hitting Jasper County at all after March.

For that matter, Bill Webster was not a fixture in the county either, but all political candidates have to have money and that and a special celebration brought Webster back to Carthage on Sept. 16. That is a night I will never forget, and the reason for that had nothing to do with Webster.

By this time, Webster was a candidate on a downward spiral. Before the primary election, polls indicated he would trounce Carnahan if he were the Republican nominee. Polls had also shown Blunt would have beaten Carnahan. But to Jasper County political observers, it was Roy Blunt's violation of President Reagan's fabled Eleventh Commandment, "Never speak ill of another Republican," that sunk Bill Webster's chance to become the first governor from Carthage.

It wasn't Blunt who caused Webster's downfall, but Webster, and it wasn't Blunt who got the ball rolling (though he certainly helped), but the *St. Louis Post-Dispatch*.

Reporter Terry Ganey, now with the *Columbia Tribune*, revisited the events in a Jan. 13, 2004, Post-Dispatch article:

"The son of an influential state senator, Webster was nearing the end of his second term as the state's attorney general. Many predicted he would become governor and then go on to play an even bigger role in national politics. Webster had high name recognition, favorable ratings and a campaign treasury bulging with money.

"But some of the "smart money" flowing into Webster's campaign was also dirty money. It came from a group of greedy and dishonest lawyers in St. Louis. One of them, Morris Kessler, was Webster's largest contributor. Another, William Roussin, raised campaign funds for Webster.

"Roussin had hitched his star to Webster's. 'It seemed like he was going places, and I thought I would go with him,' Roussin said later.

"As they gave thousands of dollars in campaign contributions to Webster, Kessler and Roussin defrauded a multimillion-dollar workers' compensation fund that Webster's office was supposed to defend.

"It was called the 'Second Injury Fund.' The scandal it created ended Webster's political career and led to federal criminal convictions of eight people, six of whom went to federal prison. Webster did, too, on other federal corruption charges."

The investigation was well underway even as Webster continued his quest to become governor. That quest brought him to Leggett & Platt at Carthage ostensibly to celebrate his 40th birthday, but more likely because Leggett & Platt consistently contributes more to Republican politicians than any other business in the state.

The event, billed as "Bill's Birthday Barbecue" was held outside the Leggett facilities, which are located just west of Carthage near Brooklyn Heights.

As usual, I wrote two stories about the event, starting one like this:

"Bill Webster cut the cake, John Hancock played ragtime piano and David Steelman smiled and waved." I probably started it that way to let everyone know that Republicans can be talented people.

It was the fourth straight year the birthday barbecue had been held and approximately 800 people were there. As people from Jasper County and all over southwest Missouri for that matter went through the line getting their brisket, baked beans, and potato salad, Hancock entertained them with some of the tunes he had played when he had worked at Silver Dollar City years earlier.

Of course, the menu included more than barbecued beef and the side dishes since it was Webster's birthday celebration. The white layer cake was trimmed with red and blue, the colors Webster had used throughout his campaign. In red lettering across the center of the cake was written, "Happy Birthday, Governor Webster!"

As Webster cut the cake, my old friend Bill Pierson from Granby (now Joplin) and his band played "Happy Birthday" and the crowd sang along.

As usual, I did not get an interview with Webster that night, but I did talk with his campaign manager. "We expect to raise more than $100,000 here tonight," Tony Feather told me. "That, coupled with the $300 to $350,000 the campaign expects to pick up at a St. Louis fundraiser tonight should put us well on our way to having what we need to beat Mel Carnahan."

Webster's primary campaign funds, some of which the Post-Dispatch articles, followed up later by the *Kansas City Star* and, of course, the Blunt campaign, had considered to be dirty money were gone. To defeat Roy Blunt and Wendell Bailey, Webster raised more money than any candidate in Missouri history. "That money's spent," Feather said. "We're just now getting started on raising money for the November election. We had a year and a half to raise the money for the primary election. Now we have only two months."

The speech Bill Webster gave that night was probably the best I ever heard him give. For a few brief moments at the beginning of the speech, when he talked about the school desegregation cases, he reminded me of his father.

In January 1989, when I was still at the *Lamar Democrat*, Sen. Richard Webster talked with me about those cases. The biggest difference between the Websters was the quick and ready sense of humor the older Webster had. During that interview, Webster said, "I've insisted all along that we really need to have Jasper-Newton County desegregation. I'd love to have those Indians from Seneca on the Carthage football team." Of course, then as now, the Seneca Indians were one of the top high school football teams in southwest Missouri. After the joke, Webster strongly criticized Judge Russell Clark's desegregation decisions, which diverted money from outstate schools in a misguided attempt to desegregate St. Louis and Kansas City schools. (The goal was good, the execution was horrible.)

Despite the lack of humor, I could see glimpses of the elder Webster in his son for the first time that night. "If pouring money into a school system guaranteed its success," Webster said, "then we would have the finest school in the United States in Kansas City. After one billion dollars in desegregation money has been put into the Kansas City school system, test scores there are going down."

Webster continued, "The school has a 50 percent absentee rate. I don't think that would fly in the Webb City School District." The attorney general went on the attack. "Mel Carnahan's solution was in his television ad. I should have paid for it. He said, 'I'd just end it.' Carnahan wants to settle with the district.

"The Kansas City and St. Louis school districts want a blank check. If you surrender, there would only be two school districts in the state of Missouri instead of 540. Settling is not the way we need to go. We can only be successful when we deal from a position of strength."

Webster was on a roll. "When Mel Carnahan ran for lieutenant governor in 1988, he had a press conference and said he wanted to be a full time lieutenant governor. He has been spending most of his time working at his law practice in Rolla, padding his bank account."

Webster then ripped into Carnahan's record as Missouri's drug czar. "After a six-week study, he had the most amazing report I have ever seen. He said there was a problem but it didn't look like there was anything we could do about it."

Webster paused, then added, "Don't tell that to the Highway Patrol," and he recited a short list of the successes the Patrol had with drug busts along Missouri's interstates.

The attorney general concluded his speech with a plea to get out the vote in the Carthage area. "If all the state was like southwest Missouri, I'd just go fishing. I would not have won the primary without the support I received from Barton, Newton, Jasper, and Lawrence counties. It was close, but the 70 to 80 percent margin in these counties made the difference. You made it possible for us to go on to the next round."

When Webster finished his speech, he was surrounded by possible contributors and I was unable to get to him. I had my story and I needed to get back to the office so as Bill Pierson's band began playing again, I listened for a while, since I have always loved his big band sound then I headed to my car.

Just before I reached the car, I heard a female voice calling "Randy Turner." I looked around and at first I didn't see anyone, but then I spotted the bandleader, Bill Pierson's wife Willi. Her real name was Wilhemina Pierson and she was the daughter of Dr. Charles O. Chester, Granby's only physician for years and years and the man who brought me into this world. (Somehow, no one ever held it against him.)

It had been a while since I had seen Willi. When I was growing up, she was working for her father at his Granby clinic, which I had to visit on a regular basis due to my asthma. When I reached my teen years, Willie, knowing how much I loved to write, saved her copies of *Writer's Digest* for me and I have read the magazine to this day.

We talked for a while about how she and Bill were doing and then she told me she always kept up with what I was writing at The Press and how proud she was of me. She said I needed to come see her and Bill sometime and I told her I would. After another five to 10 minutes of conversation, I left.

Every couple of years I would run into Willi and the result was always the same. She would tell me it had been far too long since she had seen me and I needed to stop by and see her and Bill. I always told her I would, and I genuinely intended to make that visit … but I never did.

It wasn't long after Bill Webster's birthday party that I received the news that Willi had died after a bout with cancer.

Sometimes, good intentions are just not enough.

◆   ◆   ◆

Bill's Birthday Barbecue was the last election event I attended, though the election was still almost two months away at that point. One revelation after another came out about Bill Webster's dealings with the Second Injury Fund and with his campaign contributors, and by the time November rolled around, the question was not whether Webster would become Carthage's first governor, but when was he going to be indicted.

No plans were made to send me to Webster's election night bash, and I never brought up the topic. I covered an area school board meeting that night as Mel Carnahan was elected governor.

Eventually, Bill Webster was sentenced to two years in a federal prison in Colorado. On the day his sentence began, *The Carthage Press* ran a full-page retrospective, with me writing the article and photographer Ron Graber gathering the photos and doing the layout. I took the reader through the rise and fall of Carthage's native son. The photos included the one of Webster and David Steelman at the primary victory party, one of Webster cutting the cake at Leggett & Platt, and my favorite—without a doubt—we were the only newspaper in the state to run a photo of a teenaged Bill Webster, wearing a tie that resembled a lightning bolt, taken the night he was elected Carthage Senior High School Prom King.

From Prom King to prison, the promise of Bill Webster went unfulfilled.

◆   ◆   ◆

Looking back on the election of 1992, it is hard to keep from speculating about how things could have been different. If the media had jumped on Bill Webster's problems earlier, Roy Blunt would likely have been the Republican nominee and probably would have beaten Mel Carnahan in the general election, though there is no guarantee that would have been the final result.

Had Blunt served two terms as governor, the plane crash that took Carnahan's life might never have happened. Would Matt Blunt have worked his way through the House of Representatives to secretary of state to the governor's mansion, or would he have taken a shot at the Seventh District Congressional seat after Mel Hancock retired. Remember that Roy Blunt's chief competition for the position was current Sen. Gary Nodler, R-Joplin. Matt Blunt would have been extremely young for the position, but then again he was the second youngest governor in state history.

Would a defeat for governor have ended Mel Carnahan's political career or simply put him at the front of the line a few years earlier for the U. S. Senate job he won posthumously in 2000?

Imagining what would have happened is entertaining, but in the end it does not accomplish anything. That being said, 1992 was a fascinating year for Missouri state politics.

ANDERSON GUEST HOUSE FIRE

It was the kind of story that propels a small town into a statewide and nationwide spotlight and for all of the wrong reasons.

On Nov. 27, 2006, a fire roared through a one-story building on the east side of Business Highway 71 in Anderson, Missouri. By the time area fire departments had extinguished the blaze, the building, a 24-year-old structure used as a group home for the mentally ill, was only a charred shell, and 10 of the 34 people who were in the building had lost their lives. Another one, who was taken to an area hospital in critical condition died a few days later, bringing the death toll to 11.

On the face of it, the events that occurred in the aftermath of the Anderson Guest House fire show the positive things that can be accomplished following a tragedy. The news media, led by Melissa Dunson and Jeff Lehr at the Joplin Globe, and John Ford at the Neosho Daily News, began to unravel the horrid record of Joplin River of Life Ministries, the organization that operated the Guest House, as well as similar facilities in Joplin, Carl Junction, and Carthage.

Missouri Governor Matt Blunt almost immediately called for the installation of sprinkler systems in group homes, and legislation to the effect was filed by Rep. Kevin Wilson, R-Neosho, whose district includes Anderson. Wilson worked tirelessly on the legislation during the 2007 session and it was passed and signed into law by Blunt.

Many positives came out of the horrific deaths of those 11 people, but some items have been overlooked by many in the media.

The media had its chance to stop Joplin River of Life Ministries even before it came into existence and only sheer laziness on the part of the media and state of Missouri allowed this company to exist and allowed 11 lives to be lost.

On the day the Anderson Guest House burned, I suggested that the media turn its attention to Robert Dupont, who appeared to be pulling the strings for his wife, Laverne, who was listed with the Missouri Secretary of State's office as the person in charge of Joplin River of Life Ministries.

Dupont, Joplin, is a convicted felon, having pleaded guilty in federal court on Feb. 13, 2002, to a charge of conspiracy to defraud the United States. Dupont was the primary target in a 22-count indictment issued June 15, 2000, alleging a health care fraud scheme involving several residential care facilities, thousands of claims, and more than 200 patients, according to court records. How in the world did the Missouri Department of Health and Senior Services allow such a man to have any connection with a group home?

Government prosecutors said Dupont and others, including his stepdaughter, Kelly Liveoak, charged certified patients as homebound and submitted false claims to Medicare and Medicaid.

Though the Missouri secretary of state's office's corporation documents for Joplin River of Life Ministries, do not list Dupont anywhere, three members are listed on the Ministries' board of directors … and two of them are Dupont's wife, Laverne.

Joplin River of Life Ministries' president, according to the 2006 annual report is listed as Calvin Wheeler, 716 Lexington Avenue, Webb City, an address which has also been listed as the home address of Dupont's stepdaughter, convicted felon Kelly Liveoak.

But problems with Robert Dupont and his string of Guest House group homes should have been stopped well before Dupont ever had the opportunity to cheat the government. My newspapers, *The Carthage Press* and the short-lived, but feisty *Lamar Press*, had totally exposed problems with the Guest House operations that should have prevented Robert Dupont from ever having any connection with group homes.

◆   ◆   ◆

A young woman named Cathleen Erin Purinton, better known as Cait, administered what should have been the final rites to Dupont during a hard-hitting series that ran in both Press newspapers in 1997.

During the 1980s, needing manpower to help provide news coverage for the Lamar Democrat, Publisher Doug Davis had given me the go-ahead to start an intern program for high school students and occasionally for college students. Many of those who worked for the Democrat during that decade went on to successful journalism-connected careers, including Randee Kaiser, who was my sports editor at Carthage before joining the Carthage Police Department, Amy Lamb, later the lifestyles editor for The Press and a reporter for the Independence Examiner, Peggy Brinkhoff, who worked for Country Music Weekly, Kari Wegener, who held a key position at O'Sullivan Industries in Lamar before its demise, Mary Lou Newman, now an assistant Jasper County Clerk, Cherie Thomas, who has been successful writing grants for Kansas school districts, and Holly Sundy, who has been the Lamar High School journalism teacher for more than a decade.

After I left for The Carthage Press in 1990, Doug Davis continued the program and one of those whom he hired was Cait Purinton. On her first day as a teen reporter for the Lamar Democrat, Cait was sent to Barton County Circuit Clerk Jerry Moyer's office to get information on the biggest story in the city at that time ... the case against a young woman who gave birth to a baby and abandoned it in a restroom at O'Sullivan Industries.

I was making my rounds at the courthouse at the same time and had the chance to talk with her. She was clearly out of her element at that point, but with her eagerness and obvious intelligence I had no doubt Cait had the makings of a good reporter.

During the latter part of her senior year at Lamar High School, Cait wrote me a letter asking if I had any summer employment opportunities at The Carthage Press. I told Jim Farley this was one young woman we needed to hire and he gave me the O.K.

Cait worked for us two summers. She did a series of solid articles and features during the first summer, but it was during that second summer, the summer of 1997, that Cait hit her stride and the story that put her on the map was a beating at the Lamar Guest House, owned by Robert Dupont and Karl Householder.

Cait wrote: "Mitchell Henry was found in his room at the Lamar Guest House face down on the floor in a puddle of his own vomit June 9. His clothes were soaked with urine and his face was stuck to the floor with the dried vomit, according to Division of Aging documents. (The Division of Aging was the forerunner of the Department of Health and Senior Services.)

"It was Henry's beating which apparently had happened more than 24 hours earlier that led the state to begin the investigation that eventually led to the Lamar Guest House's closing. He had been beaten by 17-year-old Matthew Wolff in an argument over a cigarette. Woolf had been placed at the Guest House as part of condition of his parole. He had a history of multiple criminal arrests, a past of explosive behavior and inappropriate sexual behavior, according to Division of Aging documents.

"The Guest House took on Wolff though it had no one on its staff trained to deal with someone with Wolff's needs, putting the other residents at risk, according to the documents.

"The beating resulted in two Class I violations, the most severe handed out during state inspections.

"At the time, Paul Shumake of the Division of Aging told Cait "it could be a lifetime sentence (not being able to operate homes in Missouri) if it there is abuse or neglect to a resident."

That would have been enough for a good story, but I recommended that Cait check to see if Dupont and Householder owned any other facilities. She took the suggestion and began digging, getting her hands on every state document she could.

One thing Cait found was that Division of Aging officials seldom communicated with each other. It was Cait who ended up telling them that the same people who had problems in Lamar, were the ones who had a facility in Butler closed. You might have thought the state agency would have checked into any other homes owned by the same company (which at that time was Sandhill, Inc.), and the same people, but that was not the case.

The near-fatal beating of Mitchell Henry at the Lamar Guest House might have been prevented had the Division of Aging closed the facility after it closed the same company's facility in Butler, the Butler Guest House, in May 1996.

Cait found this description of the Butler Guest House in state inspection reports:

"In the rooms, the windows can't be easily opened, the rooms are filthy and disorderly, and the windows are dirty with smoke residue, dust, and fingerprints with dead insects lying in the window sill.

"As the residents of the care facility wander down the corridors, they see brown buildup of dirt along the floor with grease and debris growing on the dust. The original gray linoleum floor now has a brownish cast to it due to the floor being littered with food debris and dirt.

"The dining room and kitchen where the residents receive all their meals, are not any different from the rest of the facility. The ice machine is covered with white stains, red stains, and food debris. The pass-through window counter located between the dining room and dish washing room is covered with food debris. And the only place to sit is on the metal chairs heavily soiled with food and grease. The residents' rooms and bathrooms are dirty and unkempt in several degrees of severity. More food debris or dirt is on the floor, cigarette butts and ashes are all over the floor and window sills, the beds are unmade with dirty sheets and insects are found crawling the walls and light fixture covers. Dusty brown cobwebs climb the walls and ceilings. Dirty clothes are thrown about the rooms and the baseboards are filthy with dust."

The inspection included 43 pages of deficiencies, which were not addressed properly and eventually led to the closing of the facility

But there was more to Sandhill, Inc., and the Guest House operations than the Lamar and Butler operations. Not only was the Division of Aging unaware that the same company had problems at two different facilities (the explanation given was that the facilities were in two different regions of the Division of Aging indicating that there was almost no communication between officials in the various regions), but it was also blissfully ignorant that Sandhill was violating the regulation that requires group homes to be financially solvent. This is a critical requirement since companies with financial problems have a tendency to cut corners, something that could cost lives.

Barton County Recorder Jean Keithley showed me a tax lien that had been filed with her office that showed Sandhill had declared for bankruptcy. A quick check with County Treasurer Frances Cato showed Sandhill had a bad habit of never paying county taxes.

I passed along the information to Cait, who called Shumake at the Division of Aging. During her conversation with Shumake, Cait asked about Sandhill's bankruptcy. The question was followed by a long silence. Finally, Shumake admitted he was unaware that Sandhill had declared bankruptcy. It turned out he was also unaware the company had not paid its county taxes.

Following up on the bankruptcy information, Cait uncovered another Guest House operation with serious problems. Cait's investigation discovered the company's aborted attempt to open a Guest House in Springfield, an attempt which Dupont claimed led directly to the bankruptcy.

"The city of Springfield refused to issue necessary local licenses," company officials claimed in court documents. Sandhill sued the city of Springfield claiming discrimination against its clients because they were mentally ill. The city closed the Guest House in Springfield, claiming it was not properly zoned. The closing caused cash flow problems and caused Sandhill to default on some of its debts.

◆   ◆   ◆

The Lamar Guest House was also hit by the fire bug, according to Division of Aging documents. On March 17, 1997, in a small upstairs room, a resident piled paper and combustible materials and set a small spark that grew into a fire. He

panicked and left the room. The Guest House was evacuated, but after firefight-
ers had the blaze under control, they found a woman asleep in her room. A tragic
situation was averted, but things could have been far worse. A Dec. 16, 1996,
inspection of the Guest House showed the fire alarm had been silenced, problems
existed with the emergency lighting, the facility did not have the proper amount
of fire extinguishers, the smoke separation barrier code had been violated, and the
fire alarm panel was not functioning properly.

It wasn't as if Dupont and Householder were not aware of what could have
happened. Between 1994 and 1997, four fires had been set at the Lamar Guest
House. In one of her articles, Cait noted, "According to the documents, the basic
structure of the facility creates a situation in which the building could burn rapidly if a fire occurred."

"At the time of a previous fire, a fireman said he did not know why the building did not burn to the ground," the inspection report said.

As Cait pored over the documents, she discovered fire problems everywhere.
"Problems have escalated with aggressive residents and residents who do not follow the smoking rules set at the facility," she wrote. "One resident was found in
her room asleep with a cigarette in her hand that had burned down."

The inspection report said, "The facility has not provided supervision to prevent harm to this and other residents, nor have they followed their own policies
which are present in each incident report."

The state allowed Sandhill to get away with one violation after another from
1993 until it finally closed the Lamar Guest House in 1997, as one of Cait's articles in the July 11, 1997 *Lamar Press* revealed:

"The Lamar Guest House is not meeting the needs of the residents required
by the regulation that every resident is to be clean, dry and free of offensive body
and mouth odor.

"Checks by the Division of Aging included the finding of five residents who
smelled of perspiration and body odor, were unkempt with oily, uncombed hair
and were wearing the same clothes for more than two days in a row.

"According to one resident's records, a psychiatric evaluation and care plan
suggested her caregivers bathe and shampoo her hair. Inspectors found her hair to
be oily and uncombed.

"Another resident was reported to have such foul odor 'his room smelled and
his route about the facility could be traced by his foul odor,' according to the
documents."

Cait's article noted roaches were found all over the Lamar Guest House in inspections in 1994, 1995, and 1997.

Cait Purinton did a remarkable piece of reporting, one which was recognized by the Kansas City Press Club as she received an investigative reporting award, the only award ever won by *The Lamar Press*. It would be nice to say that her brilliant investigative work led to the closing of the Guest House facilities. Only one, however, the Lamar Guest House, closed as a result of Cait's tenacity. The name Sandhill, Inc., passed into history and Robert DuPont continued to expand on his Guest House empire.

A large part of the responsibility for that oversight, no doubt, belongs to the state of Missouri's Division of Aging. I have always believed the media also contributed. If the same kind of pressure had been placed on the Division of Aging in 1997, as the *Joplin Globe*, the Joplin television stations, the *Neosho Daily News*, and other media outlets as the pressure put on state officials after the Anderson Guest House fire, 11 lives might have been saved. No one ever picked up on the story and it was far easier for the state to close the Lamar Guest House and simply forget about the wanton way in which Robert Dupont and Karl Householder ignored and took advantage of state regulations that were designed to protect the people.

It would be easy to say that the passing of nine years between the closing of the Lamar Guest House and the Anderson Guest House fire made it difficult to foresee what might have happened, but the media did not connect the dots even when the clues were right in front of them.

Just as the state was blissfully unaware that Dupont's company had filed for bankruptcy protection in the 1990s, it also failed to note that he filed for bankruptcy a second time in 2004, something that was only mentioned in *The Turner Report*.

Though Dupont had already been convicted of fraud at that time, he still listed his job as executive director of River of Life Ministries. The Guest House locations in Anderson, Joplin (2), and Carl Junction were listed as belonging to Dupont.

At that time, he owed $57,500 to the Internal Revenue Service, and $120,100 in fines connected with his fraud conviction. In another court case pending at that time, he was being sued by Land Purchase of Jasper County, which he owed $370,000, according to the bankruptcy court documents. He listed $994,000 in assets with $975,000 of that coming from real estate, and $1,419,675 in liabilities.

According to the bankruptcy court documents, at that point Dupont not only served as River of Life Ministries' executive director and pulled down a salary of $60,000 plus, but he also charged the not-for-profit organization $12,000 per month rent, with $11,400 going to the bank and the other $600 to Dupont.

The bankruptcy petition was later dismissed with Dupont and his wife filing a document saying they "would prefer to pay their creditors off on their own."

Until the Anderson Guest House fire, the state never bothered to check and see if these Guest Houses with connections to a man who had twice filed for bankruptcy, were financially solvent.

As much information as Cait uncovered in the 1990s, and I dug up from bankruptcy court records a few years ago, action was finally taken after the media onslaught that followed the Anderson fire. Apparently, it takes 11 deaths to get the media to take notice.

WORKING TOGETHER TO SAVE LIVES

As almost always happens in times of tragedy, public figures all say the right things. They promise that nothing like this will ever happen again and they will leave no stone unturned in their efforts to protect the citizens.

Such was the case with the Nov. 27, 2006, Anderson Guest House fire.

Governor Matt Blunt, who toured what remained of the facility following the fire, penned the following words in a column distributed statewide on Jan. 5, 2007:

"The tragic fire at the Anderson Guest House on November 27 is a reminder that our state must do everything possible to protect those who cannot always protect themselves. On that sad day 11 innocent lives were lost in that horrific tragedy.

"After touring the remains of the facility and visiting with first responders I ordered the Departments of Health and Senior Services and Mental Health to immediately assess and review all safety laws and regulations related to residential care facilities. I asked the departments to report to me with recommendations on enhancing safety at our state's residential care facilities by the end of last year. They presented a very thorough report to me on December 29th.

"Their report solidified my belief that sprinklers are an appropriate first step to enhance safety. I am calling for sprinkler systems in all long-term care facilities and have directed the Department of Health and Senior Services to create a time-line to implement the new sprinkler regulations to allow facilities time to meet the new requirement. Current state regulations require sprinklers in all facilities opened after October 2000. According to figures contained in the report more than half of our state's facilities lack sprinkler systems, which is simply unacceptable.

"Also unacceptable is any instance of abuse or neglect. Last month I signed an executive order to ensure that every instance of abuse or neglect in our state's mental health system is reported and investigated and those who commit these heinous acts are held accountable.

"The Department of Mental Health will continue to inform the Missouri State Highway Patrol and local law enforcement officials of any deaths or assaults occurring in a facility that is operated, licensed or certified by the department, and further states that the department must report all deaths in a facility to the local coroner or medical examiner.

"The order also directs the Department of Mental Health to implement an information management system that can quickly and effectively track critical information on abuse, neglect and other information related to the safety of individuals in public mental health facilities and in the care of private community providers. To help families whose loved ones are patients at Missouri's mental health facilities, the executive order requires the Department of Mental Health to develop individualized training for families on identifying and reporting suspected cases of abuse or neglect.

"My prayers go out to the families and loved ones still suffering from the tragic events at the Anderson Guest House. Our state must learn from this devastating event and ensure that we are doing all we can to protect the vulnerable."

It was Rep. Kevin Wilson, R-Neosho who picked up the ball and ran with it on the legislative front, sponsoring HB 952, which called for the following:

> "This bill requires all long-term care facilities licensed by the Department of Health and Senior Services to install and maintain approved sprinkler systems in accordance with the National Fire Protection Association by August 28, 2007, and be equipped with a complete fire alarm system by August 28, 2010. In addition, all long-term care facilities licensed by the department after August 28, 2007, must have electrical systems installed and maintained in accordance with NFPA 70, National Electric Code, by a qualified electrician. The department may require employees and contract personnel of any long-term care facility to be awake, dressed, and prepared to assist residents in case of an emergency and the facility to have an emergency preparedness plan." The Electrician/Sprinkler System Installation Statewide Qualification Commission, which expires July 1, 2008, is established to study and review development of a statewide standard for persons practicing as electricians and persons installing or inspecting sprinkler systems. Members of the commission will include the directors of the departments of Health and Senior Services, Economic Development, and Public Safety and persons appointed by the Governor including one individual who has been practicing as an electrician for the preceding five years, one individual who has been practicing as a sprinkler system installer or inspector for the preceding five years, a member of a local jurisdiction for electricians or sprinkler system installers, two representatives from the relevant skill trade organizations, and one public citizen. The commission must submit a report to the Governor and General Assembly

with recommendations in support of or opposition to statewide standards by July 1, 2008."

You would think no one could argue with the necessity of Wilson's proposed legislation, but there were those who would have been inconvenienced financially by the bill's requirements. Eventually, the bill was watered down to the point where it did not apply to two-thirds of Missouri's group homes. No group homes with less than 20 residents have to comply with the requirements. Efforts were made, unsuccessfully, to increase that number to 30.

The legislation that was passed was worthwhile, but it was not what it could have been, or what it should have been. Meanwhile, as some legislators were pushing for Kevin Wilson's bill, efforts were already underway to undercut safety requirements for nursing homes and group homes that were passed in 2006, only this time the efforts were taking place behind closed doors.

Fortunately, for the public and for those who cannot take care of themselves and must rely on the kindness and compassion of state legislators, one elected official saw what was going on and leaked the information to David Catanese of KYTV in Springfield, author of the KY3 Political Blog.

In his Jan. 22, 2007, post, Catanese wrote about the backdoor machinations of Rep. Bryan Stevenson, R-Webb City:

"Stevenson is pushing a motion in a committee to strip close to two dozen Department of Health and Senior Services rules from legislation designed to regulate the residential facility industry.

"Stevenson, the vice-chair of the Joint Committee on Administrative Rules (JCAR), said his motion, 'in no way reflects his opinion of the legislation.'

"'Our committee has a very narrow focus, and that is to ensure rules and regulations fit within our guidelines. There were 120 pages of regulations. A few went beyond statutory limits allowed,' Stevenson said. 'They didn't fit in the framework of the statute.'

"'But this is not a policy debate. If a Representative or Senator wants to introduce legislation to allow these changes, that is a different story," he added.

"Stevenson's motion includes stripping language requiring background checks for workers in facilities, specific responsibilities for workers during an emergency, immunizations for residents and staffing provisions."

Catanese's exposure of Stevenson's gambit saved the regulations as the Webb City Republican backed down and cast his vote in favor of the changes, but the question remained. Why would Stevenson try to throw a monkey wrench into regulations that would improve safety and perhaps save lives.

Perhaps Stevenson is simply a stickler for detail, but there could be another explanation. An examination of campaign finance documents filed with the Missouri Ethics Commission shows Stevenson has an extremely friendly relationship with the nursing home industry.

That is evident in the disclosure report filed eight days before the 2006 general election. In this report, which was issued when campaign contribution limits were still in effect for Missouri candidates, Stevenson received maximum $325 contributions from the Missouri Health Care Association, the most powerful group representing the nursing home industry, District C of the Missouri Health Care Association, and Cornerstone Healthcare, Rogers, Ark.

Even more telling were nine contributions, totaling $2,275, received by Stevenson on Oct. 20, 2006. These included $325 contributions from the Health Care Association Good Government Fund, Missouri Assisted Living PAC, Residential Care Facility PAC, MORESPAC, Burlington Northern Railway, and the Rural Telecommunications PAC. Two hundred fifty dollars contributions were received from the Missouri Pharmacy PAC and the Missouri Community Pharmacy PAC.

Many of those names are not associated with the nursing home industry, but they have one thing in common—they are represented by one of the most powerful lobbying firms in Missouri—Gamble & Schlemeier, headed by William Gamble and Jorgen Schlemeier.

All of those contributions came one day after Gamble & Schlemeier signed the Missouri Health Care Association as a client. One of the major skills of the lobbying firm over the years has been its ability to deliver large number of bundled contributions for its biggest clients through the use of its apparent minor clients.

Two months after receiving more than $3,000 in contributions that can reasonably be connected to the nursing home industry, Bryan Stevenson, behind closed doors, made a considered, though unsuccessful, effort to gut nursing home reform.

If Stevenson's handiwork had not been exposed by Dave Catanese and his source, the reforms may very well have been completely eliminated.

THE BEGINNING OF THE TURNER REPORT

During the first three and a half years I worked at The Carthage Press, I served as the area reporter, the investigative reporter, sports reporter, feature writer, photographer, well, you get the picture. I did a little bit of everything ... and that was just the way I wanted it. For the first three years I commuted, first from Lamar, and later from Newtonia in the eastern part of Newton County, both commutes being slightly over 25 miles The reason I didn't move to Carthage immediately was simple: I was still conflicted about remaining in journalism. Though The Press had been good to me and I was making more money than I had at Lamar, I still was not getting ahead and I was already in my mid-30s. I had received some offers from some larger newspapers, but in the back of my mind I still wanted to go into teaching. By this point, a dozen years had passed since my student teaching experience at Diamond, but my love of working with young people had been rekindled during my years at The Democrat when I had the opportunity to train young reporters.

Still, without the editing responsibilities I had hit my stride as a reporter at Carthage. Skeptics had told me I would not fare well in the world of daily journalism, but I was turning out four or five stories a day and had received recognition for my work at the local, regional, and national levels, something I had never expected. Finally, in early 1993, tired of driving so much and not able to afford a new car, I moved into Carthage to save some wear and tear, both on me and my Oldsmobile. I was actively considering other possibilities, when I came across some information that eventually sidetracked my plans for the next five and a half years.

On those few occasions when there was downtime at The Press, I liked to read through some of the old articles that were stored on our aging computer system. Since everything was filed by the month, I learned quickly that you could read everything on the computer system simply by going through each month.

The good stuff—the stuff we were never supposed to see was included in the 11-11-10 file. By reading through those items, I was able to find out long before I was supposed to changes that were taking place or were being contemplated.

One night as I waited for a telephone call from a source from Carterville, I glanced through the 11-11-10 file and was stunned to find that Neil Campbell, the managing editor at The Press since 1974, was planning to leave due to ill health. As I continued reading, I also discovered that he and Jim Farley had tabbed me as the Press' managing editor.

How in the world was I going to act surprised when they broke the news to me?

Naturally, my impending promotion was on my mind, but I waited and waited for the next several days and nothing happened. The days turned into weeks and still no one said a word or even dropped a hint.

By this time, the new economics of the newspaper business had finally reached The Carthage Press, and we knew the staff was going to be trimmed, but we did not know by how much. The newsroom had seven people at that point, Neil Campbell, City Editor Jack Harshaw, Marvin VanGilder, Sports Editor Randee Kaiser, Lifestyles Editor Emily Boydston, staff photographer Ron Graber, and me. I was not looking forward to becoming managing editor at a time when the news staff was going to be cut by two, three, or maybe even four people.

Finally, after waiting for more than two weeks, when I arrived at The Press one morning, I was called into Jim Farley's office, where Neil was already seated.

As far as I know, they never had an inkling that I already knew I was going to be offered the job. By this time, I really wasn't certain they had not changed their minds. "Neil is going to be stepping down later this month as managing editor and we want you to take his place," Farley said. I was caught slightly offguard by the lack of a buildup to the statement, but Farley was never one to mince words.

I was quickly told the promotion would include a sizable pay increase. After coming to The Press three and a half years earlier at $250 a week, I would be making well over $400 a week, maybe not much money to anyone else, but quite a bit when you are used to barely making ends meet.

Then Farley hit me with the down side. "You are going to have a five-man staff and that includes you." Of course, Neil Campbell would no longer be there, but someone else had to go to get the staff down to five.

Marvin VanGilder was going to retire, Farley said, adding that VanGilder would still write editorials and a weekly column. "The five people are going to be you, Jack, Randee, Ron, and Amy Lamb." That caught me offguard, but it also made the job much more attractive.

I quickly assessed the situation in my head. The institutional memory would still be there with Jack Harshaw, and with Marvin VanGilder continuing to contribute. Randee Kaiser who had been with the newspaper since 1991, had worked for me at the Lamar Democrat. He was steady, reliable, knew sports, and was an excellent photographer. Ron Graber, since joining the Press staff the week I went to Jefferson City to cover Bill Webster's victory party in August 1992, had proven to be the best photographer the newspaper had ever had, and he had a knack for organization that eventually would make him the key to any success I had as Press editor.

The mention of Amy Lamb came out of the blue. My first dealings with Amy had come when I was at the Lamar Democrat in 1987 and was hiring young reporters. Amy, a Lamar High School junior, asked if she could work for the newspaper. I gave her a chance and she immediately turned out strong, well-written copy. I was unaware that she was younger than most high school juniors, however. Where most of them were 16 and already had their driver's licenses, when Amy started, if I assigned her to cover a school activity or a meeting, her father drove her, and she never said a word about it until later. That was how badly she wanted to be a reporter.

After working for me for two years, Amy went to the University of Missouri, and inevitably into its world-famous School of Journalism. As she drew closer to graduation, I began encouraging her to send in an application to the Press and I had talked her up to Neil. He had asked me to have her send him some clips and those clips had impressed both Neil and Jim.

Then the other side of what Jim had said hit me. "What are we going to do about Emily?"

"We're going to let her go as soon as Amy is ready to start." I knew Jim and Neil had not been happy with Emily's work in the months since Nancy Prater left The Press, but I was still hoping that this was Emily's decision. I knew it would be a few weeks before Amy could start, so for the time being I had to get as much as I could out of Emily, knowing that in a short time I was going to fire her..

I accepted the job, but on one condition—I would still be doing a considerable amount of writing. I would guess no one in that room thought I would be able to do that because of the requirements of the job, but I was determined I was not going to lose what made my work so enjoyable. I also knew that on a five-man staff, you had to have someone who could churn out multiple stories daily.

And that was the way it worked. Amy started in January and Jack Harshaw took over the police beat and worked it with the enthusiasm of a cub reporter.

We didn't miss a beat. When Jack left at the end of 1994, I began working with all young reporters and it was always invigorating. Amy served two stints at The Press, and I also worked with kids like John Hacker, now back at *The Carthage Press*, Rick Rogers, now the publisher of the Neosho Daily News, Mary Guccione, Stacy Rector, Tricia Gould, Brian Webster, Brooke Pyle, and Cait Purinton.

As I reached my 40s, I found myself working with people more than 15 years younger than I, all of whom were more skilled with computers. I was in danger of becoming a relic. It was during a time when Ron, Randee, and Mary Guccione were on my staff that I became aware of this new-fangled thing called the internet.

I watched, filled with envy, as the younger reporters talked about e-mail and different websites and I felt a bit left out and extremely old. The Internet was set up on two newsroom computers, Ron's and Randee's, since those two did most of the pagination work for the newspaper.

One night when I was the only one left in the newsroom, I decided I was going to conquer the internet. I sat down at Ron's computer. It only took me a few minutes to figure out how to connect, then I started surfing the net for the first time. It was about a quarter to seven when I began. By the time I finished, it was past midnight, and I had uncovered three stories, all of which landed on page one of the next day's Press.

"This is easy," I thought, and I looked forward to setting up daily internet beats. I was going to revolutionize small town daily journalism. Of course, it was not that easy. I didn't take into account that I was able to find those three stories because they had been there all that time and no one had been looking for them. Now they were gone. Still, I quickly grasped that the internet was going to make big changes in reporting and, on a small scale, I started making the same kind of rounds I would later make when doing *The Turner Report*. The major difference is the internet was still in its infancy at that point. As each day, each week, each month passed more and more information became available. It should have been the most effective tool small newspapers ever had. It has been useful, but few newspapers have taken advantage of the stories that are out there on the world wide web just waiting for enterprising reporters.

It was a short time after my initial voyage on the internet that I found the story that led to an understanding of the way politics work that I had never had before.

WHEN IS A LOBBYIST NOT A LOBBYIST?

It was no secret that some people did not like T. Mark Elliott, R-Carl Junction, when he represented his area in the Missouri House of Representatives, but I was never one of those people.

The things I wrote about Elliott were not always kind, but he was a politician who earned my appreciation, because he was always straight with me. If you ask some politicians a question they will ignore the question and simply parrot the day's talking points. Mark Elliott always answered the question, even if sometimes he did not appreciate the question.

Elliott also had a knack for giving quotes that sounded good in headlines or turned mundane political stories into ones that could be put above the fold on page one.

He also was able to get solid legislation through at a time when his party was in the minority in Jefferson City. One example that comes to mind came when a former employer of mine, the Diamond R-4 School District, insisted that it did not have to reveal how much it paid to settle a sexual harassment claim against a former superintendent. Thanks to legislation offered by Mark Elliott, the taxpayers had to be told how their money was being spent. Honesty was, and I am sure still is, though he is out of the political life, important to T. Mark Elliott.

However, there were a few times when Elliott was honest, he just didn't come right out and tell everything.

During July 1998, the hottest Republican primary race was in the 127th Legislative District, where the incumbent, T. Mark Elliott, was opposed by businessman Steve Hunter.

Hunter had accepted a $2,000 personal loan for his campaign and that drew Elliott's anger. On his campaign disclosure forms, in capital letters, Elliott wrote, "THIS COMMITTEE DOES NOT ACCEPT LOANS." This, of course, was back in the time before all campaign finance documents were posted on the internet. I had to get them from the Jasper County Clerk's office, since they had to be filed both in Jefferson City and in the county in which the election was taking place. As I continued leafing through Elliott's disclosure form, I came across a name that seemed familiar. It was a name I associated with lobbying.

Using the new tool I had only recently discovered, the internet (thank you, Al Gore) I quickly found a lobbyist directory and began checking it against the names on Mark Elliott's disclosure form.

The result was the first article I ever wrote about lobbyists' contributions to candidates, a subject I have continued to address on a regular basis for the past nine years.

Elliott's papers included donations from six registered lobbyists and one from a registered lobbyist's wife and none of the six lobbyists were listed as lobbyists on the forms.

Burch and Associates, which gave a $200 contribution, referred to former State Representative Jerry Burch, then and now a successful lobbyist. Among his clients at that time were the Branson Area Chamber of Commerce, City Utilities of Springfield, the County Commissioners Association of Missouri, Greene County Commissioners, Missouri Hospital Association, Missouri Optometric Association, Missouri Public Transit Association, and Southwest Missouri State University.

J. Scott Marrs, Springfield, who gave a $250 contribution, had Bass Pro Shops, Branson Area Chamber of Commerce, City of Springfield, City Utilities of Springfield, Missouri Telecommunications Association, Missouri Hospital Association and Vatterott College among his clients. Marrs' occupation was listed as "government consultant."

Mark J. Rhoads, Jefferson City, who gave the maximum $275 contribution, had a client list that included AT&T, Anheuser-Busch, the American Automobile Manufacturers Association, City of Joplin, General American Life Insurance Company, Lambert St. Louis International Airport, Leggett & Platt, Inc., Missouri Insurance Coalition, and St. Joseph Riverboat. Rhoads was also listed as a "government consultant."

Rhoads' wife, Kristy L. Rhoads, Jefferson City, who was listed as a "housewife" on the form, also gave a $275 contribution (and is now a registered lobbyist).

Another "government consultant," Brent Hemphill, Jefferson City, donated $100 to Elliott. Hemphill's clients included the city of Joplin, General American Life Insurance Company, Missouri Telecommunications Coalition, Missouri Insurance Coalition, Missouri United School Insurance Coalition and St. Joseph Riverboat.

Randy Scherr, Jefferson City, whose occupation was listed as "executive direc-
tor," was also a registered lobbyist, whose client list included Lambert St. Louis
International Airport, McDonald's, Missouri Association of Criminal Defense
Lawyers, Missouri Library Association, Missouri Organization of Defense Attor-
neys, Prudential Insurance Company, RCA Mutual Insurance Company, and
Southwestern Bell. Scherr chipped in with $250.

Jeff Leeka, Joplin, was listed as "district manager," which he was, for Empire
District Electric Company of Joplin, but he was also a registered lobbyist representing the company's interests. He donated $375.

Elliott won the primary election and despite my writing that story and another
one that mentioned the lobbyists who donated to his campaign under disguised
job titles, he never held it against me, at least as far as I know.

When the world of journalism left me in 1999 and I finally took the plunge
into teaching, one of the first guest speakers I asked to come to my creative language arts class was T. Mark Elliott.

He held the students' interests with a mock debate over a proposed law. And
despite strong lobbying by a group of students who favored strawberry ice cream,
Elliott guided the class through the steps to make chocolate ice cream its official
dessert.

Unfortunately, other politicians who have done their best to disguise their
connections to lobbyists, have not been as high-minded and ethical as T. Mark
Elliott.

THE HUNTER AND THE HUNTED

It's hard to remember a time when Rep. Steve Hunter was the man speaking out against corruption in politics, but that's the way Hunter, who for the past six years has served in the Missouri House, began his career.

In 1998, he came to The Carthage Press office speaking of how he wanted to return the House seat held by T. Mark Elliott to the little people. "I want to be the man who represents the little people, the workers, the small businesses," Hunter told me, and I was touched by his sincerity. I believe that was his intention when he made his first foray into elective politics. He lost to Elliott, but he made it clear he was not discouraged.

Two years later, Hunter a pharmaceutical salesman and former schoolteacher, was elected to the House when Elliott chose not to seek re-election. By the time Hunter took office in January 2001, I was in my second year of teaching at Diamond Middle School. And thanks to a strange bit of gerrymandering engineered by Elliott, Diamond was included in the 127th District.

While teaching a unit on the Missouri Constitution, social studies teacher Grant Reed asked Sen. Marvin Singleton to speak to his class. Singleton was unable to fit it into his schedule, but asked Hunter to fill in for him. While not as engaging as Elliott was during Elliott's speech to my class a year earlier, Hunter was informative, forthcoming, and provided a considerable amount of useful information despite his limited time in the House.

Grant Reed and I talked to him for quite a while after the final class dismissed and again, I was impressed by his sincerity and willingness to serve the people. It wasn't long, however, before Jefferson City's special interests came calling on Steve Hunter.

As I noted before, I had already left journalism and was teaching when Steve Hunter joined the House of Representatives, but thanks to the miracle of the internet, I found I was able to do something I had never dreamed would be possible. I was able to take up investigative reporting, something which I had always enjoyed, as a hobby.

My first, short-lived effort came in 2000. During the spring, an eighth grader at Diamond Middle School, Chris Wall, was talking to me after school and suggested that I start a website. "I don't have the time," I told him, and he responded, "I can have one set up for you in an hour."

I was skeptical, but curious. As I anticipated, Chris was dead wrong … He had me online in less than 30 minutes. That initial website, done on Homestead, received exactly 100 visitors during its entire six-month existence. Depending on what items I include nowadays, *The Turner Report* sometimes has more visitors than that in an hour.

During the summer of 2000, I established two websites, the original *Wildcat Central*, a website that provided news about Diamond Middle School and the Diamond R-4 School District, and my first Turner Report website. Both were hosted by Tripod. During the two-year existence of that website, I dipped back into reporting, mostly following cases in federal court, or updating stories that I had covered while at Carthage and Lamar, including the first mention of the federal charges against Guest House owner Robert Dupont, but for the most part no one was reading it and it was difficult to update. I had never heard of blogging technology at that point.

It was something I suggested during my teaching role that brought me back into investigative reporting. I had two Diamond Middle School eighth graders, Michelle Nickolaisen and Alicia Bradley, with outstanding writing ability that I thought could use one of the oldest outlets for such abilities … writing journals of their everyday activities. When I made that suggestion, they took to it immediately, but they did so in a manner which I had never imagined. They began posting their private thoughts online. It was the first time I had ever heard of blogging.

I did not immediately start a blog, but I gave it careful thought over the next few months, as I continued to do most of my writing on *Wildcat Central*. The decision to create a blog came after I began working at South Middle School in Joplin in the fall of 2003.

Why I did this, I do not know, but I made a promise to my first communication arts (English) classes at South, that since I was going to make them write every day, I would do the same thing. At first, I accomplished that by working on my class website, www.room210.com or *Room 210*, also done on Tripod. In November 2003, I decided to try blogging.

My first blogging entries were mostly comments about school, books I had read, movies I had watched, or reminiscences of newspaper and school days. I never thought seriously about turning the blog into a news and commentary site.

The change occurred gradually, starting with a few items in August 2004, and then continuing to build from there. The availability of more government documents and more news information sources on the web made blogs like *The Turner Report* possible.

So I changed the blog from being mostly personal commentary about things happening in my life and news events to finding items that were not being covered by the local media (and sometimes even regional and state media). My first foray into the lobbyist disclosure forms filed with the Missouri Ethics Commission came on Friday, Sept. 24, 2004. I began scanning through the documents late Friday and since school was not in session the next day I kept looking and was surprised when I examined the reports concerning Steve Hunter. Apparently, the little people, the workers, and the small businesses had been replaced by the special interests.

His most persistent suitor, according to 2004 Missouri Ethics Commission documents was a lobbyist named Sarah Topp. Ms. Topp works for the fabled Gamble & Schlemeier firm, which represents a number of interests, including Ameristar Casinos. Apparently, Steve Hunter felt the necessity to take a number of fact-finding missions concerning Ameristar.

Where most of Hunter's colleagues manage to keep a limit on the amount of gifts they receive from lobbyists, Hunter has consistently ranked among the top two or three in such gifts each year and has, on occasion, accepted more than any of his colleagues.

The records indicated Hunter accepted travel expenses from Ms. Topp on three occasions through the first eight months of 2004. He accepted travel expenses from lobbyist William Gamble one other time. The records indicated Hunter's trips were courtesy of Ameristar Casinos, which had only recently moved its operations into Missouri.

On Jan. 22, Hunter accepted $91.32 in travel expenses, according to Ethics Commission records. He also accepted $91.32 in travel expenses, indicating he most likely went to the same place, as well as $125 for meals, food, and beverage from Ms. Topp on Feb. 20, $138 in travel expenses from her on March 8, and $455 for meals, food and beverage on March 20.

Hunter accepted an additional $250 in travel expenses from Gamble on Aug. 28, according to the Ethics Commission records. Hunter was the only legislator to receive gifts from Ms. Topp in February and the only representative (there were three senators) who received gifts in March, records indicate.

The $1,150.64 Hunter received from the gambling interest was more money than any other Joplin area legislator received from all lobbyists' gifts combined. And the gifts just kept coming.

Ethics Commission records indicate Hunter had received "meals, food, and beverage" from a number of lobbyists on a fairly regular basis. These include:

—$84, Jan. 22 from William F. Waris and Ginger Steinmetz. Waris represents a number of health concerns, while Ms. Steinmetz was a lobbyist for the city of Joplin.

—$9.60 the same day from Michael Goessling, another lobbyist for health and insurance companies.

—$65 Feb. 17 from James Kistler representing Associated Industries of Missouri.

—$43.69 March 2 from Kent Gaines, who represented Premium Standard Farms and Monsanto, among other interests.

—$124.16 on Feb. 18, and $67.26 on March 16 from Tom Rackers, who represented insurance interests.

—$30 March 30 from Kyna Iman, Missouri Southern State University lobbyist.

—$55.96 April 13 from Samuel Licklider, Empire District Electric lobbyist

—$35.50 the same day from David Martin, also representing Empire District.

—$64.50 April 26 from Greg Johnson, an insurance lobbyist.

—$46.38 May 5 from Daniel Mehan of the Missouri Chamber of Commerce.

—$70 May 14 from Randy Scherr, city of Joplin.

Hunter also received $120.20 for "entertainment" from John Kristan Jones, an MCI lobbyist, on June 24, according to Ethics Commission records.

With the legislature in session for approximately 75 days between January and early May, Hunter received gifts of "meals, food, and beverage' from lobbyists on 30 days. Apparently, Hunter, in the middle of his second two-year term was completely unable to resist the lure of freebies from almost any special interest.

As far as I can determine, the posts on the gifts Hunter received from lobbyists were never mentioned in any other news source other than *The Turner Report*. But those apparently made a difference. As word spread about Hunter's Ameristar Casino-sponsored excursions, suddenly the reports submitted by Gamble & Schlemeier's lobbyists changed. It is rare, if ever now, that you will see any travel, meals, or other gifts paid for by Ameristar Casinos alone. Now nearly all gifts are spread among multiple Gamble & Schlemeier clients. It is almost impossible to tell which special interest is actually paying for a trip or a meal, and the online reports filed by the lobbyists do not include details about the destinations for trips, where the meals are eaten, or other information that taxpayers have every right to know.

In October 2004, I noted that Hunter had received $2,852.86 worth of gifts from lobbyists, according to the Missouri Ethics Commission. Of that total, $1,832.68 came from lobbyists who listed Ameristar Casinos as one of their clients.

Hunter explained his policy on accepting lobbyists' gifts during a 2005 interview with Susan Redden of the *Joplin Globe*. "Hunter, a former pharmaceutical salesman, said lobbyists' expenditures 'are no different than the dinners and gifts I used to buy for doctors and their staffs.' "Of course, there was a considerable amount of difference. Hunter was not elected to his position by the special interests, but by the voters of his district in Jasper County, most of whom would never even think about influencing his vote by buying him a gift, a meal, a drink, or paying for him to go on some fun-filled junket. What Hunter apparently never considered was that most of his constituents were brought up better.

Hunter argued the point in his interview with Ms. Redden. "All it does is get you in the door," Hunter said. It does a lot more than that.

It gets them in the door and makes sure that someone is listening to them. If all it did was get them in the door, then you would not be seeing so much money spent on lobbying and you would not see so much money contributed to political campaigns.

If all it did was get them in the door and they didn't see any results from it, they wouldn't be doing it.

If lobbying didn't pay off for the special interests who engage in it, then why on earth, for instance, does the Missouri Hospital Association, which hit a home run with the legislation to limit the awards in medical malpractice lawsuits, have 23 registered lobbyists, including the governor's brother Andrew Blunt?

But while Steve Hunter was averaging approximately $3,000 a year in lobbyists' gifts, he found a way to make the association even more profitable. In 2003, Hunter went to work for a lobbying organization, and suddenly the seemingly aimless Hunter, who had offered little in the way of legislation during his first few years in the General Assembly, now had a purpose.

THERE'S NO BUSINESS LIKE BIG BUSINESS

The first three years of Steve Hunter's legislative career were marked by the filing of only a few non-descript bills.

In 2001, the rookie legislator filed only two bills. HB 1012 was designed to restrict the sale of precursors to methamphetamines, while HB 1018 would have established a Health and Safety Fund and the Healthy Missouri Trust Fund to handle distribution of tobacco settlement money. Both bills received hearings, but neither advanced.

Hunter's results in his second year in the legislature were much the same. Again, he submitted two bills. Again, neither bill made it out of committee.

One bill would have slightly amended requirements for the sex offender registration list. Anyone supposed to be on the list would have been required to register by Sept. 10, 2002, and register with 10 days of moving into a county. Hunter's other bill would have exempted pension and retirement benefits from state income tax.

Things began to change for Hunter in 2003 as he began his second term. He was appointed Chairman of the House Workforce Development and Workplace Safety Committee. He sponsored three bills, and for the first time, had one which was business-related—a bill that would have revised prevailing wages for construction workers. It was Hunter's first bill in his three-year legislative career to make it out of committee. Of course, it was his own committee. The bill was never voted on by the full House.

Another bill would have exempted food sales by religious and charitable organizations from sales tax. The bill received a hearing in the Agriculture Committee, but never left the committee.

His third bill would have made manufacturing a controlled substance within 2,000 feet of a school a Class A felony. The bill was referred to the Crime Prevention and Public Safety Committee but never received a hearing. Hunter's 2003 member biography read "In addition to his legislative duties, Rep. Hunter is in sales."

His 2004 biography read the same, but Hunter's status had already changed. Three weeks after the end of the 2003 General Assembly, he found a new job as a membership recruiter for Associated Industries of Missouri, a powerful pro-business lobbying organization. And that is not just my term for it. AIM spells out exactly what it does on its website. It represents the "interests of Missouri employers before the General Assembly, state agencies, the courts, and the public." In other words, it is a lobbying organization.

Financial disclosure forms filed by Hunter with the Missouri Ethics Commission indicate that he was employed by Associated Industries of Missouri from 2003 on and received at least $1,000 each year. Unfortunately, all officeholders are required to state on these forms is if they received more than $1,000; they do not have to be specific as to the amount.

Missouri Ethics Commission records show that in 2003, Hunter received $216.25 in gifts from Associated Industries lobbyists, including $112.60 on four dates in October and November, well after he began working for the organization.

The expenditure reports show Hunter received $8.81 for meals, food, and beverage from lobbyist James W. Kistler on Nov. 13, 2003, as well as $65 in travel from Kistler on the same date. Hunter had another $21.72 for meal, food and beverage from Kistler two days later. The expenditure forms show an $8 meal from Kistler on Nov. 12 and a $9.07 meal from him on Oct. 22.

Other dates on which the Joplin legislator received gifts from Associated Industries lobbyists during the 2003 session were:

Jan. 21—$35.75 for meals from David Smith

April 9—$26.23 for meals from Smith

May 1—$31.59 for meals from Smith

May 21—$10.08 for meals from Gary Marble, Associated Industries president and a former Republican state representative from Neosho

Those gifts were among the $2,025.17 Hunter received from lobbyists during the 2003 calendar year, again ranking him among the top legislators in that category.

It would be safe to speculate that if Steve Hunter was not the chairman of the House Workforce Development and Workplace Safety Committee he would not have been the first person AIM would have thought about hiring. Although Hunter did not file any legislation that would necessarily benefit his second employer in 2004, that changed the following year.

In 2005, Hunter filed three anti-union bills which went nowhere.

House Bill 876 would have required that unions disclose the following information: Assets, including cash, accounts receivable, loans receivable, U. S. Treasury securities, investments, and other assets; liabilities including accounts payable, loans payable, mortgages, and other liabilities; cash receipts from sources including dues, fees, sales, interest, rent, and dividends; cash disbursements including negotiation, administration, organization, lobbying, political, benefits, overhead, gifts and contributions, membership status including active, inactive, associate, apprentice, retired, and others. The bill smacked of 1950s McCarthyism.

House Bill 877 would have established "employee rights" according to the wording on the bill. It would have prohibited any requirements that people join unions, pay dues or fees to unions, and would eliminate any current agreements between unions and employers that violate those rights. This back-door approach would not only have made Missouri a right-to-work state (which does a lot for employers and not much for workers), but it would have enabled employers to get rid of contracts they have already signed, but do not like.

House Bill 878 would have required that no money be spent on political activities unless it comes "from a fund established for that purpose." Under the provisions of that bill, unions would be required to notify members that they do not have to contribute and that nothing will happen to them if they do not. Of course, businesses would have been allowed to continue to contribute to any politicians or political causes they wanted to, especially to elected officials who continue to add to the businesses' profits by sponsoring this type of legislation.

Though the anti-union bills were unsuccessful and have been in the past two years, as well, Hunter struck gold with a bill to make it more difficult for employees to receive workmen's compensation. The anti-union bills went nowhere, but the workmen's compensation bill became law.

Perhaps Hunter wrote every word of the bill himself. He is certainly an intelligent man. But it would not be a stretch of the imagination to believe that AIM staff could have been very helpful in constructing the pro-business legislation.

Hunter sponsored that bill as a representative for this area, then put on his other hat after the end of the legislative session and spoke at eight "Lunch and Learn" presentations put on by Associated Industries across the state, speaking as an AIM employee to explain what he had done for the organization as a legislator.

A few months after Hunter began his other job, reporter Aaron Kessler of the *Joplin Globe* asked him if the new job didn't present him with a conflict of interest. "I don't see it as a conflict of interest at all," Hunter told The Globe, adding he would not benefit "one iota" from his position as a state representative.

"We're citizen legislators, not full-time," Hunter told the newspaper. "I'm like an outside salesman (for Associated Industries). It's not a conflict."

As for what kind of salary Hunter received from his other job, he would not tell The Globe during that September 2003 interview and neither would Associated Industries President Gary Marble, who told the newspaper, "I'd rather not discuss that."

Marble added, "I'm comfortable everything was legal … pure as the driven snow." Marble would know about that, having gone directly from being a state representative for the Neosho area to being president of one of the most powerful lobbying organizations in the state.

Hunter's second job screamed conflict of interest from the first time it was revealed, and though the Globe ran with the story after it was first revealed in the *St. Louis Post-Dispatch*, Hunter's 2004 member biography, as mentioned previously, makes no mention of his work for Associated Industries.

The first official mention came in the 2005 biography, which said, "In addition to his legislative duties, Rep. Hunter is a membership recruiter for Associated Industries of Missouri and works for an advertising company."

Hunter abandoned all pretense of his jobs being separate entities during a series of speeches following the 2005 legislative session. From May 17 to May 26, 2005, Hunter criss-crossed the state, as the featured speaker and a number of "lunch and learn" presentations for Associated Industries. It was more of a victory lap.

Hunter's final presentation was held in Hannibal, following appearances May 17 in Springfield, May 18 in Joplin, May 19 in Kansas City, May 20 in Jefferson City, May 24 in St. Louis, and May 25 in Cape Girardeau.

The media helped Hunter continue his double duties for more than three and a half years. With only a few exceptions, Hunter's status with Associated Industries was not mentioned when articles were written or stories aired concerning his pro-business legislation. Hunter received a free pass from Joplin-area media after a couple of early mentions.

Ironically, during the 2007 legislative session, Hunter filed a bill that would have made it illegal for members of the General Assembly to work for lobbying organizations. The bill description read: "This bill prohibits members of the General Assembly from being employed by or under contract to any organization engaged in lobbying." The bill was assigned to Hunter's Workplace Development and Workplace Safety Committee where, naturally, nothing else was ever done with it.

Despite the disappearance of HB 1149, Hunter was not finished with public comments on conflicts of interest. On May 29, 2007, Missourinet reported Hunter hit State Auditor Susan Montee with accusations that Ms. Montee's claim in her audit of the Division of Workmen's Compensation that the fund would be millions of dollars in the hole next year was colored by the fact that her attorney husband represents people who try to receive money from the fund. That is a legitimate subject to explore, but Missourinet and other media sources that picked up on the story made no mention of Hunter's conflicts of interest involving the workmen's compensation issue.

Of course, there could have been a lot more to the equation. Not long after Hunter blasted Mrs. Montee, Governor Matt Blunt fired the Director of the Division of Workmen's Compensation, Pat Secrist, and Hunter resigned his job with Associated Industries.

A few short weeks ago, the big rumor around the state capital was that the next director of the Division of Workmen's Compensation would be Steve Hunter, a man, of course, who has no conflicts of interest. That did not pan out, as Governor Blunt appointed a party hack to the position.

CITIZEN LEGISLATORS?

In an ideal world, the people we send to Washington or Jefferson City would put the needs of their constituents first and foremost, not just the needs of the special interests who contribute money to their campaign war chests. The lobbyists roam the halls at will in our nation's capital and at Jeff City. Though the doors are open for average, ordinary citizens to visit most legislators, it is difficult to find the time to drive to the capital. So how do legislators determine what their constituents want?

One way is through annual surveys, which are generally worded in such a way that the respondents are going to answer questions the way the legislators wants them answered. For instance, "Do you believe our children should be sent to the best school possible?" Well, who would not answer "yes" on a question like that. Legislators then wave these phony surveys to show that constituents support educational vouchers, knowing that if vouchers are thrown into the equation many of those positive votes would switch to the other side.

Many legislators use surveys to prove support for their own beliefs. If there is as question in which the special interests that pay the freight for their campaigns are going to have different views from the constituents then that question is not going to find its way onto the survey.

Our senators and representatives also attend numerous city and county celebrations and parades, which gives them a chance to be seen as supporting the community, but do not offer much of an opportunity to hear the voters' concerns.

There is one segment of local voters who always have the ear of legislators across the state. Our elected officials really think they are hearing what the average voter thinks when they attend the Chamber of Commerce "Eggs and Issues" breakfasts or legislative luncheons. Is it any wonder so much legislation is geared toward the business interests? Of course, there are the people who have the money to keep the spigot flowing.

I have attended more of these functions than I care to remember. I have heard more talk about efforts to protect employers at the expense of workers. At one time, I wondered whether these elected officials would make the same comments if they were speaking to a group of workers, and I quickly realized they would not. They wouldn't be caught dead speaking to a group of workers.

For many legislators, and my experience, of course, has primarily been with the ones in southwest Missouri, their business is business, but sometimes it's a bit more parochial than that. The Missouri General Assembly is fraught with examples of legislators who have sponsored or co-sponsored legislation that benefits them directly.

A prime example of this occurred shortly after pre-filing of bills for the 2007 session began. Rep. Ron Richard, R-Joplin, who as this book is being written is one of two candidates for Speaker of the House, pre-filed a bill which I picked up on quickly. At the time, it was the only bill he had pre-filed, which, fair or not, gave constituents an idea of what his legislative priorities were.

Any businessman who serves in the legislature is probably going to be involved with various bills that could have an effect on their own business, but Richard took it one step further.

HB 150 apparently came after a long investigation by Richard into what issues concerned the residents of the district he serves in Jasper and Newton counties. Consider this segment of the bill, which specified a certain area Richard believed deserved to be exempt from sales tax:

"all purchases of equipment, machinery, materials, supplies, fixtures, and shoes by the owner or operator of a facility used for the sport of bowling where sales tax is collected and remitted on all amounts charged for participation in such sport, including amounts paid for the rental of items used to participate in such sport."

How does this affect Richard? Consider these items from his website:

1991 to present

Full duties with C & N Bowl Corporation. (He operates five bowling alleys.)

1988

Additional duties of Vice President and Secretary of C & N Bowl Corporation, Senior Managing Officer responsible for overall activities over five Bowling Centers in two states. Assumed further duties associated with financial side of operations and planning.

1987

Duties were added of Chief Financial Officer of two Joplin, Missouri, locations, Ft. Smith, Arkansas, and two Little Rock, Arkansas bowling locations.

1985 to 1987

Bowling Center Manager of new facility, Carl Richard Bowl East, Joplin.

1978 to 1987

Assistant Financial Officer of C & N Bowl Corporation.

1971

Joined C & N Bowl Corporation as Assistant League Coordinator and Food and Beverage Supervisor.

1965 to 1971

During high school worked in all areas of Bowling Centers including construction, janitorial, maintenance, sales and service; U.S. Post Office, processed mail and unloaded trucks.

Richard has served in various capacities on the Legislative Committee of the Bowling Proprietors' Association of America, including currently serving on that organization's Legislative Committee.

This was one time the media followed the lead of *The Turner Report* and within one day Richard had withdrawn this bill, which clearly benefited only him and a few others.

On Dec. 20, 2006, an Associated Press article contained the following passage:

"Richard said he decided to wait and see what tax policy changes Gov. Matt Blunt proposes next year and determine if his bowling tax break idea fits in. But he said he sees no problem with proposing a law exempting bowling alley owners from paying state and local sales taxes on purchases for their business even as he runs a bowling company.

"'I guess it indirectly would help me,' he said. 'I don't care about all that. I'm chair of Economic Development (Committee). Anytime I can help small businesses stay in business, I'm in favor of that. If it turns out to be controversial to keep Mom and Pop doing business, that's OK with me.'"

Richard's feeble attempt to take the offensive left one question unanswered. If the legislation was not designed to benefit him, why start with bowling alleys? Was Richard that arrogant or did he just not think anyone would be looking?

◆   ◆   ◆

Ron Richard's rise to prominence in the Missouri House of Representatives makes that story of particular interest at the moment, but he is far from being the only elected official to use the process to benefit his or her own interests.

When Sen. Chris Koster, R-Harrisonville, (now D-Harrisonville as of this writing) sponsored a bill in the 2006 session that would curb Medicare and Medicaid Fraud, it had wide support. After all, this followed a 2005 session in which the Republican-led legislature had trimmed thousands of poor Missourians from the Medicaid rolls.

Koster's legislation was explained in an article in the May 3, 2006, *St. Louis Post-Dispatch*:

"Under the Senate-passed bill, Missouri would set up a system similar to one in Texas. Passing the bill, called a state False Claims Act, would put Missouri in line for federal financial incentives. So far, at least 16 states have taken that step.

"Sen. Chris Koster, R-Harrisonville, sponsors the bill. He noted that last year, the state cut 90,000 low-income people from the Medicaid rolls. He said the state had an obligation to scrutinize providers, too.

"His bill would provide that whistle-blowers—insiders with information about cheating—could receive 20 to 35 percent of the money recovered. Tipsters could file civil suits, which would be sealed while the attorney general investigated the allegations.

"Whereas some states let whistle-blowers proceed with suits on their own, Koster's bill would provide that only cases chosen by the attorney general would go forward.

"Koster told the House committee that the whistle-blower provisions were the key to getting federal incentive payments.

"The federal government pays 60 percent of Medicaid's costs, so it usually takes 60 percent of funds recovered. But if the state passes a False Claims Act, the federal government would split the bounty with the state 50-50.

It was a win-win situation for the state, but not for the one man who dealt the death blow to Koster's bill after it made it way through the Senate and reached the House—there was no way Rep. Rob Schaaf, R-St. Joseph, was going to let this bill pass.

Schaaf, the chairman of the House Special Committee on Healthcare Facilities, stood in the way of the legislation even though the leader of his party, Governor Matt Blunt, called for the reform in an op-ed published in the Aug. 7, 2006, *Springfield News-Leader*:

"I have called on the General Assembly to pass strong legislation targeted specifically at Medicaid fraud to build on the $139.7 million in savings we have already uncovered. The Senate has already passed strong anti-fraud legislation to give the state the same tools as the federal government to fight Medicaid and Medicare fraud. The legislation's opponents claim the bill, which I support, is too harsh. How can you be too harsh on those who knowingly commit fraud, steal from taxpayers and rob our most vulnerable from assistance they truly need? One phony argument made by opponents is that the bill will go after well intentioned doctors who make a mistake. This is not true. The legislation is clear that we are going after only those who knowingly commit fraud."

Despite the governor's reassurances, Rep. Schaaf remained adamant in his opposition to the legislation. Of course, Rep. Rob Schaaf has another title he sometimes goes by—Dr. Rob Schaaf.

Schaaf used his committee during the summer of 2006 to build opposition to any such bill, holding hearings in which one handpicked doctor after another testified about the harm such a bill could cause. Schaaf continued his push with this news release following the hearings:

"Jefferson City—Physicians, long-term care providers, and billing specialists painted a dire picture before the House Special Committee on Healthcare Facilities yesterday. Most indicated no opposition to finding ways to prevent Medicaid fraud. However, healthcare providers said if legislators don't exercise caution in crafting and passing Medicaid fraud legislation, they and many of their associates would be compelled to leave the Medicaid program or the state, exacerbating an already acute access problem for Missouri's needy citizens.

"Several physicians have left the Medicaid system already or no longer accept new Medicaid patients because of the program's relatively low reimbursement rates and excessive bureaucracy. The added risk of an overly broad and excessively punitive fraud measure would only compound the struggle to attract and retain the physicians needed to maintain Medicaid services in Missouri.

"'It's hard for physicians to [stay] in the program in the first place,' said Dr. Charles Van Way, Truman Medical Center Chief of Surgery. 'A major threat like this is going to push a lot of them out.'"

"Physicians noted Medicaid reimbursement rates, ranging from 11-35 cents for every dollar of care given, provide a significant disincentive for staying in the Medicaid program. The disincentive is so great that specialists are opting out of taking Medicaid patients, creating a serious access problem.

"'There's a shortage ... in the greater Kansas City area of specialty care for Medicaid patients,' said Dr. Robert Gibbons, president of the Metropolitan Medical Society for Greater Kansas City.

"Lack of access isn't limited to medical services. Dr. Matt Niewald, a dentist in Lee's Summit indicated that children could have to wait weeks and travel up to two to three hours for dental care through Medicaid.

"Those testifying took issue with proposed legislation, including provisions that would crack down on honest mistakes—like entering in a billing code one digit off of the correct code—and that would give undue incentive for whistle-blowers without imposing a penalty for filing a frivolous charge. They also stated that the inclusion of a private cause of action, which allows private attorneys to bring suit on behalf of the state and was included in the Senate version, would line trial attorneys' pockets while inadvertently lessening access to medical care people need.

"In the wake of their concerns, healthcare providers indicated support for a more refined approach. In the words of one physician, rooting out provider fraud is like cutting out cancer: you do it "with a scalpel ... not a bludgeon or a meat ax." First, participants were fairly unanimous in their call for legislation that punishes those with clear intent to defraud and protects those who make honest mistakes. Some believed whistleblower incentives would poison doctor/patient trust. Others believed they would be helpful. Most expressed support for suits filed through the attorney general, not private attorneys. The committee's chair, Rep. Rob Schaaf (R-St. Joseph), believes input from the hearing will help the committee find middle ground on fraud legislation.

"We heard a lot of fear on behalf of Medicaid patients," said Rep. Schaaf, "that they would be hurt if we're not careful. Having heard that makes me more hopeful that we can convince the Senate that we can work together to craft a bill that would be helpful without hurting Medicaid patients."

And, in the end, a workable compromise is the hope not only of the committee but also of Speaker Rod Jetton (R-Marble Hill) who spoke to the committee prior to the beginning of testimony.

"The last thing we want to do is pass a fraud bill that causes [doctors] to drop out of the program or quit seeing [Medicaid] patients," said Speaker Jetton, "because that would be detrimental to the folks who need those services ..."

Dr. Schaaf's counter-strike against the Medicaid fraud legislation could very well have more behind it than just his medical license. Missouri Ethics Commission records indicate most of his campaign money comes from the medical community.

At the time Schaaf's committee held its hearings, its chairman had received more than $10,000 in campaign contributions from medical sources in just six months. In his April 2006 disclosure report, Schaaf said he had received $8,826 in contributions, Of the 30 contributions he received, only three, a $1,000 contribution from the Buchanan County Republican Central Committee, $300 from a restaurant owner and $300 from AT&T were from non-medical sources.

Schaaf picked up $7,225 from medical sources including the maximum $300 from the Missouri Society of Anesthesiologists, Professional Medical PAC, Missouri Medical PAC, Clayton Dermatology, Digestive Disease Specialists, Serenity Women's Healthcare, Supporters of Health Research and Treatments, Tri-County Medical Society, and Western Anesthesiology Associates, Inc. The other donations came from individual physicians.

In his January quarterly filing with the Ethics Commission, Dr. Schaaf reported $6,000 in campaign contributions, with at least $3,500 coming from medical sources, and quite possibly more since some of those who donated were listed as "retired."

Schaaf's fellow physicians and the medical community did not forget the St. Joseph doctor's contributions to their well-being. During the remainder of 2006, Schaaf received an additional $9,875 in campaign contributions from physicians, hospitals, and the like, making his grand total for 2006 approximately $20,000 ... and this was before campaign contributions were removed.

The eight days before primary disclosure form filed by Schaaf on July 30, 2006, lists $3,625 in contributions, all of them coming from medical sources, most of it in the $325 maximum increments that were required at that time.

On his October 2006 disclosure form, Schaaf reported an additional $2,975 in contributions from the medical community, including the following: Missouri Health Care Association, $325; District 3 Missouri Health Care Association, $325; District 2 Missouri Health Care Association, $325; District 1 Missouri Health Care Association, $325.

Eventually, Medicaid Fraud provisions were included in SB 577 during the 2007 session, but with enough compromises that Schaaf was not only able to support the bill, but also shepherded it through the House. Unfortunately, in one of those problems that seems to come up with every piece of legislation that goes through either chamber, Schaaf ran into an opponent who had to be placated during the negotiations on this legislation—Rep. Charlie Shields. While Schaaf was looking out for the interest of himself and his fellow doctors (you won't see many of Schaaf's patients contributing to his campaigns), Shields also had a horse in the race.

As the *Kansas City Star* reporter Kit Wagar noted in the opening paragraph in a May 2007 article about the fight over the new state Medicaid program:

"The chief protagonists are Rep. Rob Schaaf, a St. Joseph Republican and a family doctor, and Sen. Charlie Shields, a St. Joseph Republican who works for Heartland Health System, which operates hospitals and manages a health insurance plan.

Who is representing the needs of the patients?

MISSOURI'S FIRST FAMILY

My memories of Roy Blunt had always been positive ones since his appearance at the Lincoln Ladies Ice Cream Social. At that time, I pictured him as an honest, gutsy politician who had no qualms (at least none that could be seen) about stepping into a place where he knew he was not wanted, and telling people things they did not want to hear.

I followed Blunt's career after his loss to Bill Webster, through his short-lived presidency at Southwest Baptist University in Bolivar, until he defeated Gary Nodler in the Republican primary and went on to replace the retiring Mel Hancock as Seventh District Congressman. I knew he was a conservative Republican, and I didn't necessarily have any problems with that. I considered him an honest man and at that point, I thought of him as the man who probably should have been governor of Missouri if Bill Webster would have had the good sense to drop out of the race when he realized that the revelations about his extracurricular activities were going to put him in a federal penitentiary.

The first inkling I had that the Washington Roy Blunt was different from the Roy Blunt I remembered from 1992 came in July 2004 and that information was what led me to change The Turner Report from the hodgepodge collection of anecdotes and movie and book reviews I had done up to that time, into the more hard news-driven website it is today:

It was also the first time that I discovered that one of my prize possessions, a 1998 Christmas Card from Congressman Blunt with a photo of him, his wife Rosann, sons Matt and Andrew, daughter Amy, and daughter-in-law Melanie was a Norman Rockwell portrait of a family that no longer existed.

I read the Joplin Globe and the Springfield News-Leader every day and I had no idea of the changes that had taken place with my old friend Roy Blunt since he arrived in the nation's capital to represent my interests.

I started my July 30, 2004, post this way:

"Southwest Missouri's Seventh District Congressman Roy Blunt received a bit of unwanted national attention this week from the investigative reporting magazine Mother Jones.

"In its annual awards for legislators who misuse or abuse their positions, Blunt was a nominee in the category of 'The Heidi Fleiss Medal for Congressional Pandering.'

"Quoting from the magazine, 'Rep. Roy Blunt became House majority whip in November 2002; hours later he secretly slipped into the 475-page bill creating the Homeland Security Department a provision benefiting Phillip Morris USA. Blunt's language would have restricted low-cost cigarette sales on the Internet and prosecuted contraband sales. The congressman receives massive donations from Phillip Morris; his son works for Phillip Morris; and he recently married the Washington lobbyist for Phillip Morris. After the outrage was discovered (so outrageous that ethics purist Tom DeLay had the measure stripped), Blunt wailed that cigarette sales are connected to homeland security because Hezbollah has made money by selling discount smokes.'"

Knowing that Mother Jones has a liberal bent (and there is nothing wrong with that) I decided to research this a bit more. The information came from a June 2003 Washington Post investigation. That was when I first learned that the Congressman had used his Washington connections to pour money into son Matt's successful 2000 race for secretary of state, something he did again four years later when Matt Blunt ran for governor.

"The Hill," a Washington-based newspaper, used Missouri state records to show just how the senior Blunt used his position to benefit his son. According to The Hill, "Missouri state records show contributions to Matt Blunt's campaign (for secretary of state in 2000) came from firms and individuals with business pending before Roy Blunt's subcommittees. Although some of the companies have significant interests in the state, others do not.

"Top executives at Freddie Mac, for example, contributed $4,000 to his campaign. On Nov. 6, 2000, Vice President Gary Lanzara and Vice President Leland Brendsel gave $1,000 each. Two weeks later, Freddie Mac lobbyist David Glenn and his wife, Cherie, also contributed $1,000 apiece. (Note: It should be pointed out that $1,000 was the most individuals can contribute under Missouri state law at that time.) Cherie is listed as a homemaker; the couple reside in Great Falls, VA.

"Contributions from telecommunications-related entities accounted for over $10,000. Railway transportation companies also contributed more than $6,000 to Matt Blunt's campaign. John Scruggs, a top lobbyist for Altria, formerly Phillip Morris, contributed $1,000. Other contributions came from companies and executives in—or representatives for—such heavily regulated industries as healthcare, insurance, chemicals and defense technology."

The article continued, "By far, the biggest outside contributors to Matt Blunt's campaign, however, were colleagues of Roy Blunt. Campaign finance documents show 84 House lawmakers made 95 contributions to the secretary of state campaign, totaling more than $65,000.

In the article, Larry Noble of the Center for Responsive Politics, suggests logically that the donations were made, not by a desire to help Matt Blunt, but by a desire to curry favor with his father.

Political experts cited in the article said the out-of-state money that poured into Matt Blunt's campaign coffers was the deciding point in a close race. Without it, the younger Blunt would have lost.

That article was the first time I learned that Roy Blunt's son, Andy, was a lobbyist. And then when I discovered that Roy had left his wife and had married a lobbyist young enough to be his daughter? After an initial twinge of envy, I was ticked off. To me, this was a sign that the Blunt family could very well be enriching itself at the expense of Missouri's taxpayers.

And in the months thereafter, I continued to find more and more evidence to support that supposition.

◆   ◆   ◆

It did not take long for me to find that Roy Blunt and his son, the governor of Missouri, had one important trait in common—they had no problem attracting contributions from lobbyists. The senior Blunt's connections with lobbyists did not bode well for him following the Jack Abramoff scandal, but he did his best to portray himself as a leader in the battle against corrupting influences in politics. It didn't help his posturing much when the January 2006 disclosure report filed with the Missouri Ethics Commission showed the governor, Roy Blunt's son, had collected $30,000 in campaign contributions from federal and state lobbyists (not counting the bundled money he received from the same sources). The federal lobbyists, of course, could all be connected to the governor's father, including several from Cassidy & Associates, the Washington lobbying firm that employs Roy Blunt's former chief of staff Gregg Hartley and until a few days before the posting of the disclosure report, employed another of the Congressman's former staff members, Jared Craighead, who left the lobbying firm to become Matt Blunt's chief of staff.

Among the donors with federal lobbying connections were:

—Ali Amirhooshmand of Cassidy & Associates, a former Roy Blunt assistant, donated $500.

—Steve Gordon & Associates, Washington lobbying firm, maximum $1,200

—Wayne Berman, lobbyist and co-sponsor of the Tom DeLay defense fund, $1,200

—Jordan Bernstein, Alexandria, Va., lobbyist for Cassidy & Associates, and former administrative assistant to Missouri Congresswoman Jo Ann Emerson, $1,200

—Craig Fuller, former lobbyist and assistant in the Reagan White House, now head of the National Association of Chain Drug Stores. Both Fuller and his organization donated the maximum $1,200.

—Gregg Hartley, former chief of staff for Roy Blunt, now with Cassidy & Associates, $1,200

—Akin, Gump, Strauss, Hauer, and Feld, a Washington lobbying firm whose top officials include former Democratic National Committee Chairman Robert Strauss and former Clinton advisor Vernon Jordan, $1,200

—Richard Hohlt, a lobbyist for Altria, J. P. Morgan, SBC, and other interests, $1,200

—Integrated Legislative Strategies, the firm that lobbies for Daimler Chrysler, $1,200.

—Hecht, Spencer & Associates, a lobbying firm which represents among others R. J. Reynolds.

—James Hirmi, Cassidy & Associates, $500

—Matt Jessee, former special assistant to Bush-Cheney '04 National Finance Vice Chairman Jack Oliver and later an assistant to Rep. Eric Cantor, R-Va.

—Former Attorney General, U. S. Senator and Missouri Governor John Ashcroft, $1,200.

Matt Blunt's January 2006 disclosure form also listed a number of Missouri lobbyists. As the younger Blunt raised more money than any governor or candidate before him, the gravy train was being financed by the same special interests that called the shots for the Blunt administration.

◆   ◆   ◆

In his second State of the State message in January 2006, Governor Blunt touted his "Energy and Green Power Initiative." In addition to the full funding of Missouri's bio-diesel and ethanol incentive funds, the governor said, "I ask that we give Missouri's heartland economy a major and lasting boost by requiring that motor fuel sold in Missouri for passenger cars and trucks contain 10 percent ethanol."

The governor continued, "This standard will spur even greater economic development in rural Missouri. For all of us, it will provide cleaner air, lower prices and greater independence from Middle East oil supplies. Please stand with me against special interests and for our farmers, consumers, the environment and new energy supplies made right here in Missouri."

It was not the first time Matt Blunt has expressed those sentiments, and the Energy and Green Power Initiative passed easily through the Republican-controlled General Assembly.

Naturally, the governor's brother, lobbyist Andrew Blunt, was not going to let an opportunity like that pass by. It wasn't long after the governor's speech that the younger Blunt brother added a new client to his lobbyist list. According to documents filed with the Missouri Ethics Commission, Andrew Blunt signed to represent AGP, an Omaha, Neb., based firm ... which in the fall of 2006 opened a new ethanol production plant.

AGP has been a major player in Missouri politics for quite some time, according to Federal Election Commission documents. Between 2002 and 2006, the company's political action committee contributed $12,000 to Senator Jim Talent, $6,000 to Senator Kit Bond, $10,000 to Congressman Sam Graves, and $10,500 to Rep. Kenny Hulshof.

Governor Blunt's campaign contribution disclosure forms did not include any donations from AG Processing, but he had received $2,200 over the previous two election cycles from the Omaha offices of the national law firm Kutak Rock. According to Kutak Rock's website, the law firm serves as counsel "for the acquisition, construction and financing of ethanol plants."

Those revelations, which I made on my blog in February 2006, turned out to be the just the tip of the iceberg. Revelations from other media sources indicated that Andrew Blunt was a partner in a company developing ethanol plants, while a southwest Missouri ethanol plant was owned by a Blunt cousin.

◆   ◆   ◆

And then there's healthcare.

Governor Blunt and the Republican-dominated General Assembly came under fire for their actions eliminating thousands of Missourians from the Medicaid roles. One of the chief architects of that short-sighted policy was Rep. Jodi Stefanick, and the governor rewarded both her and the healthcare interests that donated tens of thousands to his campaigns by appointing her as his senior health care policy advisor.

Ms. Stefanick's campaign coffers were filled with special interest money from doctors and health care and insurance companies ... and, of course, she donated $1,200, the maximum allowed under state law, from that campaign money to Blunt's campaign.

In her last few days as a legislator, Ms. Stefanick went out in style, accepting nearly $400 in gifts from health care lobbyist James R. Moody in June, well after the 2005 legislative session had concluded, according to Ethics Commission documents.

Moody's report indicates that he spent $368.40 on June 15 for travel for Ms. Stefanick, while representing Schaller Anderson, a national health care management and consulting company. It is not clear from the online Ethics Commission documents who Moody was representing when he paid $25 for meals, food and beverage for Ms. Stefanick on June 28, but it was either for Family Health Partners or Missouri Care.

Ms. Stefanick's campaign finance disclosure forms for 2004 cement her reputation as a handmaiden for the health care special interests. While she was played a well-recognized role as a chief architect of the Medicaid Reform plan and voted for so-called reforms that helped pad the pockets of the medical and insurance interests, Ms. Stefanick received more than two-thirds of her campaign funds from the same people.

Her campaign committee's October 2004 quarterly report showed that she received at least $8,350 from health-related interests during the three-month period, including:

Missouri Hospital Association PAC for Health, $300; Missouri Hospital Association Southeast District PAC, $300; Missouri Hospital Association St. Louis District PAC, $300; Midwest Radiological Associates PC, $300; Missouri Medical PAC, $300; Missouri Association of Health Plan, $200; Dr. Jeffrey Thomasson, $300; Professional Athletic Rehab Center, $250; Michael Neidorff, chairman of Centere Corporation, $300; Golden Rule Insurance Company, $300; West County Radiological Group, Inc., $300; Dr. Charles Fuszner, $300; American Family Insurance, $300; SSM Health Care, $300; Devereaux Chiropractic and Acupuncture, $75; Jim Moody (lobbyist) and Associates, $300; The Affton LeMay Chiropractic Center, $100; Dr. Donna Manello, $100; Eric Fink, Missouri Assisted Living Association, $300; Missouri Podiatry PAC, $300; someone listed as Dr. Crosby, $100; West County Care Center, $300; Missouri Insurance Coalition, $200; Whispering Lane Health Care Center, $300; Firsthand Health Center, $100; Deanna Mueller, therapist, $100; Gerald Grimaldi, Truman Medical Center, $100; Doral Dental USA, $300; Chiropractic and Sports

Injury Center, $100; Midwest Imaging and Prevention, $100; Metro Heart Group of St. Louis, $300; Group Health Plan, $300; Donna Checkett, listed in one news story as director of Missouri Division of Medical Services, which administers the state Medicaid program, $200; Dr. Joan Pernaud, $150; Midwest Cardiovascular Center, $100; Abbel Chiropractic Arts, $75; Missouri Dental Hygienists PAC, $300.

Another huge batch of health-related donors kicked in to Ms. Stefanick's campaign in the second quarter of 2004, according to her committee's quarterly report. Among those listed:

Balanced Care for Women of St. Louis, $300; Eric Fink, Missouri Assisted Living Association, $300; Health Care Association Missouri Good Government Fund, $300; Health Care Leadership Committee State Account, $300; Joan Pernoud, $200; MD Pharmacy, Inc., $300; Missouri Orthopedic Sports and Trauma Clinic, $300; Missouri Residential Care Services, Inc., $100; Missouri Society of Anesthesiologists PAC, $300; MOPLAN Missouri Psychologists, $300; Missouri Physical Therapy Association PAC, $100; Pharmacy Solutions, Inc., $300; United Healthcare Corp $150; and Whispering Oaks Health Care Center, Inc., $300.

Three hundred dollars, of course, was the maximum that could be contributed to state representative campaigns under Missouri law Even during the first quarter of 2004, before the campaigns really kicked in, Ms. Stefanick's campaign was already depositing checks from health care interests, according to the campaign disclosure form, including $300 from Sunrise Senior Living Services, $300 from Physicians for Sound Health Care Policy, $300 from Johnson and Johnson, and $200 from the Missouri Physical Therapists Association.

While Ms. Stefanick was working to cut thousands off the Medicaid rolls, she was also helping pass and craft legislation which enriched those people who supplied the bulk of her campaign finances. And for that, the governor rewarded her with a prime position in his administration.

RELY ON YOUR BELIEFS

Seldom has a political action committee or a political leadership fund had as fitting a name as the one devised for Congressman Roy Blunt's leadership PAC—Rely on Your Beliefs.

Of course, the purpose of these committees is to build power for a politician by allowing him to collect contributions then distribute them to other candidates, who then, of course, would owe him favors and support. It was a strategy Blunt learned quickly after entering Congress and he learned it from the master—Rep. Tom DeLay. A few Missourians contribute to the committee, but for the most part the money comes entirely from lobbyists, including of course, the congressman's wife, Abigail, and son Andrew, and their well-heeled clients.

A perfect example of this comes from the May 2006 Federal Election Commission disclosure report, a report that was issued at the height of the Abramoff scandal. Out of $45,500 in individual contributions the PAC received in May, more than $40,000 came from lobbyists.

In addition to the $45,500, the PAC received $224,500 in corporate and PAC contributions during the month.

At least 20 members of the lobbying firm of Wiley, Rein & Fielding contributed $200 apiece. The firm represents Nucor, Verizon, Kansas City Southern, Qwest, Aquila, Motorola, and Gannett, among other clients.

Other lobbyists contributing to the PAC include:

—Michael Bates, lobbyist for Bell South, $2,500

—John Cline of the C2 Group, which represents Pepsi Co and Fannie Mae, $1,500

—Thomas Crawford of the C2 Group, $1,000

—Douglas Davenport of Manatt, Phelps & Phillips, which represents Bell South, $1,000

—Sarcoxie native Tony Feather of Feather, Larson & Synhorst, whose clients include AT&T, General Motors, Teamsters, and Advocates for School Choice, $1,000

—G. O. Griffith of Barbour, Griffith & Rogers, represents Bell South, Delta, GlaxoSmithKline, $1,500

—Richard Hohlt, lobbyist for Altria, Bristol Myers, Chevron, and Sallie Mae, $5,000

—Brant Imperatore of Barbour, Griffith & Rogers, $500

—Nelson Litterst, former White House aide, now working for C2 Group, $2,000

—John O'Rourke, lobbyist for Securities Funding Associates, $5,000

—Andrew Shore of Mayer, Brown, Rowe & Maw, representing Harrah's Casinos, Atlantic City Coin and Slot Service, Cottonwood Financial, State Farm, $5,000

—Karen Smith, lobbyist for Proctor & Gamble, $2,500

—John Veroneau, former aide to Sen. Bill Frist and to former Senator William Cohen, now works for Cohen's lobbying firm, $5,000

It should be mentioned that not only were none of these people described as a lobbyist in the place on the forms for employment, but no employment at all was listed.

Among the PACS contributing to the Rely on Your Beliefs PAC were: Burlington Northern $5,000, American Hospital Association $2,500, American Express $2,500, American Council of Life Insurance $5,000; American Apparel and Footwear $5,000, Capital One Associates $5,000, Cash America International $5,000, Charles Schwab Corp. $2,500, Chicago Board of Trade $5,000, Edison International $2,500, Ernst & Young $2,500, Financial Services Roundtable $5,000, GE PAC $2,500, J. P. Morgan Chase & Co $5,000, Mastercard Employees $5,000, Merrill Lynch & Co. $5,000, Met Life Employees PAC $2,500, Morgan Stanley $2,500, Mortgage Bankers Association $5,000, New York Mercantile Exchange $5,000, New York Stock Exchange $2,500, Northwestern Mutual Life Federal PAC $5,000, R. J. Reynolds $2,500, Sallie Mae, $5,000, US Bancorp $5,000, Wachavia Group $5,000.

It's also fair game to look at those who in turn receive handouts from the Rely on Your Beliefs PAC. Among those have been some of the most scandal-ridden members of Congress.

One allegedly assaulted a woman, was sued by her, and eventually settled out of court. Another sent suggestive e-mails to teenage boys who were working as House pages. A third resigned after he admitted taking bribes, while the fourth resigned and pleaded guilty to money laundering charges.

FEC documents show the Blunt PAC contributed $10,000 in 2006 to former House Majority Leader Tom DeLay, $5,000 on Feb. 15 and another $5,000 on

March 29. This was in addition to $20,000 donated earlier to DeLay's defense fund.

Florida Congressman Mark Foley missed by only one dollar receiving $5,000 from the Blunt PAC in 2006, the FEC documents indicate. Foley received $3,958 on April 28 and another $1,041 on the same day. The PAC contributed $2,000 to Foley in 2003 and made in-kind contributions of airline travel for the Congressman on two occasions in 2000, adding up to $3,976.

Two Ohio Republicans also benefited from the Blunt PAC's generosity. Robert Ney received $5,000 on March 29 and has picked up $14,000 since 1999, the FEC documents indicate, while Donald Sherwood collected $10,000 from the PAC, including a $5,000 contribution as recently as Sept. 29, 2005.

To the names of those four Congressmen, you can add a $5,000 contribution on Feb. 9, 2006, to the re-election campaign of Montana Sen. Conrad Burns, who lost his re-election battle in November 2006, thanks to his connections to Jack Abramoff.

Let's examine these Congressmen, whom you would think would share some of Roy Blunt's beliefs if the title of his PAC means anything.

Mark Foley

Mark Foley resigned from Congress after ABC News confirmed he had written inappropriate e-mails to male Congressional pages. This passage was included in a Newsweek article:

"Foley's sexual leanings were also well known, or at least suspected, by a particularly vulnerable group on Capitol Hill. Every year Congress hires about 100 pages, who can be seen in their distinctive blue uniforms scurrying through the halls, running errands for lawmakers. The pages have been embroiled in earlier sex scandals. In 1983, a pair of congressmen admitted to sexual relations with underage pages (one with a girl, one with a boy). After that, the pages were housed in a dormitory and fairly closely chaperoned. A former female page, who asked not to be identified to protect her privacy, told Newsweek that she and other pages had regularly seen Foley stop and talk to pages on the House floor and in the cloakroom, lingering with them and asking them to describe their experiences in Congress. "We just gradually figured out he was flirting with the guys," said the page. "It made a lot of the guys uneasy. He was kind of creepy."

Donald Sherwood

Donald Sherwood's problems were outlined in a recent article in the New Republic:

"In 1999, at a Young Republicans event, he met Cynthia Ore, a Peruvian-American grocery-store heiress and aspiring Hill intern in her early twenties. She was attracted to his salt-of-the-earth charm. "Guys in D.C. try to be so suave," she later recalled in a newspaper interview. 'They drive Bentleys and Ferraris. Don has a truck.'

"But, by September 15, 2004, Sherwood's country charm had worn thin. That was the day Ore called the police from the bathroom of his apartment in Hill House, claiming he had tried to throttle her. When the police arrived, Sherwood protested that he'd merely been giving Ore a vigorous backrub. The police, for their part, determined that Ore did not seem to be 'of sound mind.' A year later, after their report was made public, Ore sued Sherwood for $5.5 million, but the matter was dispatched with a settlement.

"Whether Sherwood was really choking or massaging may never be known. But the episode, while no Chappaquiddick, was pretty sordid for the Tenth. 'Nobody has any morals anymore,' one constituent lamented in the local paper. And yet, Sherwood vowed to run again."

Robert Ney

Bob Ney, who eventually resigned from Congress was another who was connected to the Jack Abramoff scandal. He pleaded guilty Sept. 15, 2006, to conspiracy and lying to Congress. He admitted to providing services to lobbyists in exchange for gifts and money. The following passage comes from the *Miami Herald*:

"Ney's downfall began in South Florida where he had used his congressional influence to sway the sale of SunCruz Casinos to Abramoff and his New York partner Adam Kidan. The SunCruz case against Abramoff and Kidan gave Justice Department officials the leverage to pressure the lobbyist to turn on other colleagues, congressional aides and politicians early this year.

"The charges against Ney are based primarily on his behind-the-scenes work for Abramoff's Indian tribal clients and for a foreign businessman who gave him tens of thousands of dollars in casino chips and cash. But the charges also include the lawmaker's unusual tactics to help the lobbyist purchase the Dania Beach-based SunCruz gambling fleet."

Tom DeLay

Former House Majority Leader Tom DeLay resigned after being indicted for illegally using corporate funds in Texas political campaigns, though the charges against him were later dismissed. DeLay was also connected with Jack Abramoff and one DeLay aide, Tony Rudy, pleaded guilty to conspiring to corrupt public officials.

◆   ◆   ◆

Though the Democratic Party has control over both Houses, little has changed about the way Roy Blunt's Rely on Your Beliefs leadership PAC operates. During the first five months of 2007, the PAC had received $346,450 in contributions. Of that amount, only $23,950 came from individuals and nearly all of those were from registered lobbyists. The remaining money came from PACS, with many having the nerve to refer to themselves as "Good Government Funds." It seems probable that in their dictionaries, "good government" is defined as the government that helps to pad their pocketbooks.

In the most recent report as this book was being written, filed in June and covering the month of May, Rely On Your Beliefs reported receiving contributions of between $1,000 and $5,000 from the following political action committees:

Aetna, Alabama Farmers Federation, Altria Group, American Apparel & Footwear, American Association of Nurse Anesthetists, American Council of Life Insurers, American Dental, American Insurance Association, AMPAC of the Chicago Board of Trade, Association of American Railroads, Automotive Free International Trade, AZPAC, BSNF Railroad, Bryan Cave LLP Political Fund, Capital One Associates Political Fund, CSX Corporation Good Government Fund, Eli Lilly & Co., Fed PAC, Freddie MAC, GlaxoSmithKline, Home Depot, Independent Community Bankers, KochPAC, Medco Health, Morgan Stanley, New York Life, Norfolk Southern Corp. Good Government Fund, Northwest Airlines, Office of the Commissioner of Major League Baseball, Raytheon, REAPAC, SIFMAPAC, T-Mobile, UBS Americas, Union Pacific Railroad, US Telecom Association, U. S. Oncology Good Government Committee, US Team, Washington Group International

During May, Rely on Your Beliefs received $126,200 from PACs and $5,950 from individual contributors, including $3,200 from lobbyists, with the other $2,750 coming from company executives.

This gives an indication of whose beliefs Roy Blunt relies on. The contributors include representatives of the pharmaceutical, insurance, medical, railroad, airlines, banking, and communications industries, and the lobbyists who represent those special interests. And while those interests do not always get their way, they are successful a considerable amount of time, and they have access to our elected officials 100 percent of the time. If they were not getting anything back from these investments, they would not be forking over millions of dollars for political contributions each year.

YOU CAN TAKE IT TO THE BANK

The title of this chapter is somewhat misleading. You can take it to the bank and often times, the bank will keep it and dig its claws into you for more.

One simple fact proves how strong the banking industry is in Missouri and in the United States … Banks are allowed to charge you for not having enough money. And when was the last time you can remember a legislator proposing a bill to stop this practice?

I can't remember one either.

Nearly all banks have policies that charge you fees if you keep less than a certain amount in your account each month. I have known of people who bounced checks simply because they did not factor in these "banking fees."

Back in the 1990s, I asked about these policies. Why punish people who are doing everything they can to make ends meet? I was told it was necessary because of the cost of handling the accounts.

"Doesn't it cost more to handle the accounts that have more money in them?" I asked, displaying just how naïve I was. I can't recall ever receiving a straight answer to the question. Of course, it costs more, but how else can you milk money out of customers who are not depositing sizable paychecks and who are not taking out large loans?

The banking industry makes sure its interests are represented in the Missouri General Assembly. The most powerful organization representing Missouri bankers, naturally, is the Missouri Bankers Association. It makes up for the lack of cleverness in its name with the way it has managed to work around Missouri campaign contribution limits for the past several years.

At a time when contributions to Missouri Senate candidates were limited to $600, MBA had no problem giving $4,000 to Sen. Delbert Scott, R-Lowry City, chairman of the powerful Financial, Governmental Organizations and Elections Committee, which, of course, handles laws that affect the banking industry.

In fact, the banking industry as a whole felt obliged to pour its resources into Scott's campaign during the last three months of 2005, according to the January 2006 disclosure report filed with the Ethics Commission.

Scott received $9,285 from banks and financial institutions, including the $4,000 from the Missouri Bankers Association. Scott received the maximum $600 each from MBA State PAC, MBA River Heritage Region PAC, MBA Gateway Region PAC, MBA Truman Region PAC, MBA Mark Twain Region PAC and MBA Pony Express Region PAC and $400 from the MBA Ozark Region PAC. Surprisingly, there were no contributions from the MBA Rat Pack or the MBA Back PAC.

Among Scott's remaining contributors were:

Rob J. Linderer, banking, Lenexa, Kan., $200; Premier Bank, Jefferson City, $100; Farmers Bank of Lincoln, $100; David Turner, banking, Jefferson City, $50; Central Bank of Kansas City, $100; The Citizens-Farmers Bank, Cole Camp, $100; Bank of St. Elizabeth, $100; United Bank of Chamois, $50; County Bank, Brunswick, $75; Bank of Odessa, $100; Sherwood Community Bank, Creighton, $50; St. Clair County State Bank, Osceola, $100; Rockwood Bank, Eureka, $100; Community Bank of Shell Knob, $100; Elaine Paxton, banking, Clinton, $100; Farmers and Merchants Bank, St. Clair, $100; US Bank, Lewistown, $50; First State Bank, St. Robert, $100; First Community Bank of the Ozarks, Branson, $100; Regional Missouri Bank, Marceline, $50; People's Bank of Wyaconda, Kahoka, $50; Scott Page, banking, $50; First State Bank, Monett, $100; CBC Bank, Bowling Green, $50; Excel Bank, Sedalia, $100; Midwest Bank Centre, St. Louis, $100; Bank of Belton, $100; Chillicothe State Bank, $50; Bank of Urbana, $100; Farmers & Commercial Bank, Holden, $50; Osage Valley Bank, Warsaw, $50; Scott Orr, banking, Columbia, $100; Citizens Bank, New Haven, $50; William Breedlove, banking, Springfield, $50; Glen Williams, banking, Eminence, $50.

All of the contributions listed above, including those made by the Missouri Bankers Association were made Dec. 13, according to Ethics Commission records.

What did the bankers receive for their generosity? From all appearances, they received a champion of their industry, one who carried the sword into battle when the evil empire Wal-Mart decided it wanted to get a foothold in banking.

When Wal-Mart made its move, Scott sponsored a bill (likely written with the help of banking industry lobbyists) to keep the company out. He explained his reasoning to an Associated Press reporter. "I'm not anti-Wal-Mart, but they're a retail institution, and historically we have not mixed the two. This is a whole sea change in the way banking and commerce is done if we allow this to happen."

In 2006, Scott sponsored a bill which would have raised the corporate surety bond from $25,000 to $100,000 for companies wanting to issue or sell checks. The bill was also loaded with other costs which would have made it difficult for any competitors for that part of the banking business to emerge.

During the 2007 session, Sen. Maida Coleman, D-St. Louis, offered a bill which would have restricted predatory lending, a practice which has been especially hurtful to those with little money. The bill never received a hearing. Sen. Coleman had sponsored the same bill in the previous session. A hearing was scheduled, but was never held.

Also, during the 2006 session, a bill to keep credit card issuers from raising interest rates to people who are at least paying the minimum amount each month was bottled up in Scott's committee and never saw the light of day.

And while it is easy to cast aspersions at those who do not manage their credit wisely, there is no question that standing behind those people who fall into credit card debt and cheering them on are bankers and other credit institutions that are using every means at their disposal to seduce the poor into getting themselves into debt.

When the poor don't come through with the payments, there are an army of legislators, backed by bankers' contributions, who are willing to take action against them.

As usual, there is no one to back the little guy. And so, even if you aren't swimming in credit card debt, if you don't have much money in your bank account, you're going to be charged a hefty fee, and no one in state government is going to try to stop it.

A CURE FOR AIDS

A buzz of excitement rippled through the church as the minister stepped to the lectern. This was not a regular worship service and the pews were filled with the cream of the crop, the best Branson had to offer.

In reality, these people were not gathered for any religious purpose, though they all had talked themselves into believing it was. The minister cleared his throat, waited for the conversations to subside, and then he introduced the evening's speaker, who then spread his own particular form of gospel to the congregation, or to be more apt, his potential investors.

For the people who heard Patrick Dallas Graham at his best, they say if he told you the world was flat, you would believe him. He was an imposing man, standing well over six feet tall, walking with shoulders slightly stopped, and his weight hovered around the 250 mark.

"My last name is Graham," he said slowly, "like the old brown crackers. I have raised several companies from start up and have sold all of those companies except the one that we have at the present time. I'd be less than honest if I didn't tell you that everything that I hope to have, I owe to the good Lord. Period. There's nothing else that I can add to that."

Pat Graham gave a brief history of his company, Conquest Labs, from its beginning in 1991. "We've turned down far more dollars on investment than we have taken in."

Graham said he had been teaching his grandchildren about the Bible, that the Christian life was the most important thing of all. "If you don't feel like you're serving number one, you better. I hope nobody noticed how polished my knees are; I've been on my knees a lot lately." He said his wife and daughter had both had cancer scares.

The audience listened intently. This select group of Branson's elite had been given a golden opportunity … the chance to get it on the ground floor of Conquest Labs, a Lamar-based company that had developed a remission product, some said a vaccine, for AIDS. For their investment, they were going to make millions.

The AIDS remission project, Graham said, was brought to him in October 1991. "I was called by a university professor of mine, a fellow that we had known for many, many years and he said I have a product that you must take over.

"I said, 'That's great, Doc. We've worked together well over the years.' And he said, 'It's an AIDS remission product.' I said, 'Did I hear you right?' That's really the first thing I asked him. I was trying to see just what his drift was because I had never worked on a human product except for test kits and experimental products. He said, 'Yeah.'"

The professor, who was in his 80s, said he had worked on the product for two to two and a half years, Graham said. "He awaked one night about 2 in the morning and he wrote down in the next 24 hours everything it took to produce a workable, viable AIDS remission product. Knowing the fame of this gentleman and his sincere Christian principles that he had always followed, I never did question him again after that."

The professor told him he came to Graham instead of a big company because "He said, 'Every time I've gone with a big company to do something, especially in my retiring years, I've been done wrong.' He said they've one way or another taken over the product." Graham said the professor indicated to him that the company officials told him they were not making any money when each of them was making about a million dollars a year.

"I want to stop and point out again, this is a gift from God. This wasn't anything that I had anything to do with the developing of. None whatsoever." Graham's audience leaned forward, some sitting on the edge of the pews as they listened. At times, Graham spoke at a tone barely above a whisper. He had this group in the palm of his hand.

"I don't want anybody to sit here and get the idea that Pat Graham is a genius or something like that. I'm an old South Iowa cow milker and I can still feed the cats with either hand and that's about where my talents lie, but we were charged with doing this and I think there is three things you need to do in a Christian life.

"I think first of all you need to stay close enough to God that you know when he is giving you a job to do and you accept the job with the understanding that you're going to complete it and you keep Him with you while you're doing it, otherwise, you're going to fail anyway.

"And that's sincerely what we've tried to do here and just so that nobody thinks I'm trying to hammer you around. I want one thing from every one of you. I want you all to pray for us because what we're doing is important. The support of fellow Christians in praying for something as extreme as what we have here, we will continue to succeed with far less obstacles than if we don't have that."

The request his friend made of him became even more important, Graham said, when he discovered the professor had cancer and was dying. "Someone had to take this over and get it completed. He died in January of that same winter."

Graham told the potential investors of the number of important scientists who were working on the project, including one from Johns Hopkins University and another from the Mayo Clinic who had been dealing with cancer patients.

"Dr. Angerman worked the last 15 years on cancer remission products and when he and I first talked he said the same production module that you guys have will someday produce a cancer remission product. So we're not talking about just an AIDS remission production. We're talking about getting enough money in our public offering to do a parallel work in cancer."

At this point, Graham was just getting warmed up. There was so much that could be done with the research, he said, that he had to be careful not to try to do too much. "We just got to be disciplined enough to not try to lick all of the calves at one time."

Graham then claimed a public offering of Conquest Labs stock was in the works and that it would eventually lead to the NASDAQ stock exchange.

Graham returned to his theme of letting only the right people invest in or work for Conquest Labs, a theme that obviously resonated with his audience. "We have a lot of unusual policies in the company. Some people have left us because of it. We don't have anyone that works for us that's a drinker. They don't use alcoholic beverages. And with the exception of the two or three that we're working on, none of them use tobacco products of any kind.

"Any time you get a guy that's out there, coming in with a hangover, going to work on something like the AIDS remission product, forget it. We want them to have clean minds and be alert every minute they are there."

Graham said he wanted to have "good Christian people" as partners so he wouldn't have to worry about keeping all the money himself. "At our house, we take what we need to be totally comfortable." He said he had only one fishing pole and one rifle. "I've got everything I need. You don't want to give it to somebody who squanders it. That's not good stewardship. So you can see why it is important to us in the early going to choose the people that we want to come in." And, of course, the people in that church were the kind of people who Pat Graham wanted to have involved in Conquest Labs.

"When we went to the patent office," Graham said, "the patent personnel out there saw what we had and this one agent said, 'I don't know how you done this but you guys are light years ahead of anybody.' The scientist looked me straight in the eye and said, 'This is a gift from God.'"

And Pat Graham was concerned that the God-fearing people sitting in front of him might have a problem with investing in a remission product to cure a disease that afflicted a large number of homosexuals and drug users.

God's gift was tested, Graham said, when news of the AIDS product got out and people who actually had the disease came to Conquest Labs. "We had secretaries that were panicky. I really had to pray about my attitude about this. At one time in my life, I didn't love those people enough and I don't condone, not one iota, of anything they do, but I know God loves them, and I know that He put me in charge of this project."

Then Graham administered the coup de grace. An added benefit of his remission product, Graham said, is that it would not work on a homosexual unless he changed his lifestyle. "It doesn't matter if it's a horse or a human, if they are too far gone, you got to let them go. If they continued in their sinful ways, it didn't work at all."

Graham told the audience what he said the doctor had told him. "He said if a local schoolhouse caught on fire and all the pumper trucks in the world come up and were pumping water on it to put it out and you get some idiot out here who comes out with a gas pumper on the back side, you're going to burn your schoolhouse down. So the guy that doesn't change his lifestyle is putting gas on his fire and it just simply didn't work. So if a guy is going to try to laugh in God's face and say, 'Ha, ha, God. We got a remission product. We can lead any lifestyle we want to and we'll just take the product every month and we'll do what we want to. You know what? It isn't going to work. They're wasting their money."

It won't work, Graham indicated, because God isn't going to let homosexuals continue their "sinful lifestyle" without punishment.

Graham had his investors. The men in that Branson church were nodding their heads as this Christian man told them that he could make them rich with this AIDS remission product. And even better than that, they could do it without rewarding sinful behavior.

Surely nobody would fall for a line like that, would they?

You would think not, but by the time Pat Graham had finished lining up his investors, he had raised more than five million dollars, with much of the money coming from Branson, including investments by the Braschlers and the Hershends of Silver Dollar City fame.

It was a roller coaster ride for the Iowa transplant, and as we well know, roller coasters have only one direction to go after they reach the top.

(Note: The information in this chapter about the meeting at the Branson church is taken directly from records on file in Barton County Circuit Court.)

THE RISE AND FALL OF PAT GRAHAM

During the late 1980s and early 1990s as I covered Lamar and Barton County for the *Lamar Democrat* and *The Carthage Press*, I had heard tales of how Pat Graham was cutting a wide swath through the area, including a number of civil suits against him, but for every detractor the man had, there was someone who stood up and talked about what a good, Christian man he was.

I would like to say I was the reporter who broke the story, but as with the earlier chapter on the Webb City Police Department, that simply was not the case. The first media outlets to bring the name Pat Graham into the news were the local television stations, whose cameras were on the Lamar square on May 23, 1995, when the Missouri Highway Patrol and the Barton County Sheriff's Department executed a search warrant and confiscated about two dozen boxes of papers and some computers. The search warrant was ordered following an investigation by the offices of the attorney general and secretary of state. After the raid took place, I went on a scavenger hunt in the Barton County Courthouse to find every document I could find with Pat Graham's name on it.

The first stop was Circuit Court Judge Charles Curless' office where I reviewed the list of items confiscated during the execution of the search warrant and the documentation filed by the Highway Patrol which caused Curless to sign the warrant. According to that documentation, Graham deposited investors' money in a number of bank accounts he controlled under fictitious names, his son-in-law David Hoyt, told the investigators.

Graham's lawyer, Steven H. Goodman, sent a fax to C. Frederick Holloway, a securities investigator for the secretary of state, saying, "It appears that there has been an unregistered offering of securities. Our initial investigation has revealed that there are over 100 Missouri shareholders with sales in the aggregate amount of about $1.5 million and that the sales to Missouri residents accounted for roughly one third of the total number of sales." The fax was dated Nov. 29, 1994, about two months after Graham's son-in-law spoke with Holloway. "On Oct. 3, 1994," Holloway wrote in an affidavit filed with the court, "I received a call from David Hoyt. Mr. Hoyt stated that CLI had taken in over $2 million in investments since about May 19, 1991, from 427 investors in 15 states. Mr. Hoyt said he believed that investor funds had been converted for personal use by Mr. Graham. He reported that Mr. Graham had purchased two homes and told investors he purchased two new labs.

"Mr. Hoyt stated that investor funds had been deposited in a number of banks under fictitious names which were controlled by Mr. Graham. Hoyt said Graham was telling investors he had obtained a patent for an AIDS remission product."

A second fax, dated Jan. 25, 1995, put any thoughts of the existence of a patent to rest. "We asked for any patent applications that had been filed by CLI and copies of any patents that have been issued. There have been no patents filed by CLI and therefore no patents have been issued."

Affidavits detailed how Graham had spent investors' money on himself and his family, including these items:

—All medical expenses for Graham, his wife, his two daughters, and their husbands

—Expenses for family members to move to Lamar

—Installation of plumbing, carpeting and heating and cooling systems, and a privacy fence for the Hoyts.

—Installation of a heating and cooling system for the home of Graham's other daughter and her husband.

—A $788 per month lease on a 1994 Lincoln Town Car used exclusively by Graham

—A $659 per month lease on a 1994 Jeep Cherokee used frequently by Graham family members.

—A $526 per month lease on a 1993 Eagle Vision used as the personal vehicle of one of Graham's sons-in-law

—A $400 per month lease on a 1994 Ford Ex-Cab used as Hoyt's personal vehicle.

—Gasoline for all of the cars

—Non-business related meals for the Graham family including a birthday dinner at Jim Bob's Restaurant

On the day of the raid, Secretary of State Rebecca Cook issued a cease and desist order, stopping any sale of CLI shares.

Among the items seized in the raid were:

—Folders and miscellaneous material that Hoyt told investigators Graham had instructed him to shred, according to a sheet signed by Shelly Land, an investigator in the Trade Offenses Division of the attorney general's office.

—One box containing records of Graham's personal expenditures from 1987 to 1991.

—A file folder titled "The AIDS Remission Project"

—A file folder titled "Internal Revenue Service."

—A schematic for a filtration facility in Branson

—Details on a settlement with the Department of Housing and Urban Development

—A folder on a meeting in Little Rock, Ark.

—Income tax returns

—The passwords to his computer, "Please" for his accounts, and "Tabitha" for payroll

—Records of money transfers and overdrafts from CLI's account at the Mark Twain Bank in St. Louis.

—A copy of a *Springfield Business Journal* article regarding CLI's ill-fated effort to establish a hog farm in the Mount Vernon, Mo. Area.

But my favorite item was an Oct. 25, 1994, letter to former vice president Dan Quayle. Though the item was on the search warrant inventory, I was never able to get a satisfactory answer as to what the letter included.

Scott Holste, who then, as now, was public information coordinator for Attorney General Jay Nixon, told me, "That is interesting, but there was a large amount of material which was seized and we can't comment on any particular item." Of course, I expected that response, but later after the case was closed, I was still never able to verify the contents of the letter, though people close to the case speculated it was simply Graham asking Quayle to speak at a meeting of potential CLI investors.

After I jotted down notes and copied a few pages from the search inventory, I walked across the hall to Barton County Circuit Clerk Jerry Moyer's office, and began thumbing through the lengthy list of court cases involving Pat Graham. After that, I checked with the county recorder's office to see if there were any state or federal liens against Graham.

I found more than two dozen lawsuits and documents that indicated the U. S. Government won a default judgment in U. S. District Court, Southern District of Iowa, against Graham on July 28, 1982 for $407,130.33 in unpaid taxes. That judgment had still not been satisfied as of July 6, 1994, when U. S. Attorney Stephen L. Hill Jr., Kansas City, filed a tax lien on Graham's property.

In a document filed in Barton County Circuit Court, Marcia McAuliffe, an investigator in the Trade Offense Division of the attorney general's office summed up how Graham dealt with the lawsuits. Out of the two dozen cases, she said, "only one of those suits or judgments has been satisfied.

Among the cases filed against Graham:

—A Pittsburg, Kan. dentist was awarded $1,500 plus interests on April 24, 1984, for dental work done on Graham's daughter two years earlier.

—Gordon Jewelers, Grandview, won a $3,504.39 judgment against Graham July 2, 1980. Graham defaulted on payments on a two-diamond ring, a five-diamond wedding ring, a one-carat loose diamond wedding ring, a one-carat loose diamond and three lockets.

—E. R. Squibb and Sons, a credit firm, sued Graham's businesses, Professional Biological Laboratories and Grand Laboratories, Inc. in 1983 and won a judgment for $4,188.42. The company successfully garnisheed Graham's Lamar bank accounts, helping it recover $80.18, the total amount in his Barton County State Bank account and $44.75, the total amount in his Lamar Trust Company account.

In case after case, Graham was sued, lost, but never paid a cent. He was not the defendant in every lawsuit, however. On June 10, 1985, Graham filed suit against R&S Chevrolet, Joplin, seeking reimbursement for damage done to his 1981 Buick Skylark and 1978 Chevrolet van when the company repossessed them.

In his petition, Graham said he had "suffered emotional distress and had been exposed to public contempt and ridicule" because of R&S Chevrolet's activities. The case was dismissed on Dec. 16, 1985.

Even as Graham was collecting millions in sales of Conquest Labs stock, he continued to have problems paying his debts, according to documents filed in Barton County Circuit Court. Tonya Ehrsam, who worked for Graham from Sept. 21, 1993, to Oct. 27, 1994, told Shelly Land, an investigator for the attorney general, that she had taken many calls from "various persons wishing to speak to Graham about money he owed them."

It wasn't just creditors who had problems, Ms. Land wrote. "(Ms. Ehrsam) said that her July 1994 paycheck from CLI was returned for insufficient funds. When she confronted Graham with that fact, she said he told her he had wired money into CLI's account to cover her check. She said this was not true and that he finally met her outside the Bank of Minden where he kept his personal account and paid her in cash."

Bank records examined by Ms. Land indicated that a large transfer of money from CLI's account into Graham's account at the Bank of Minden took place shortly before the May 23 raid. At the end of April 1995, the account contained $43,144.29. As of May 17, she said, it only contained $37.20.

Ms. Ehrsam told Ms. Land that during the 13 months she worked for CLI, the company had only $250 in income, a rebate. The rest of the company's money, she said, came from investors, who had been told CLI was working on the AIDS remission formula.

After my examination of the records in the Barton County Courthouse, I drove by the house that records indicated he had purchased with investors' money. It was not an opulent mansion; it blended in with the surrounding houses, nice comfortable homes in a crowded residential section of Lamar. I snapped a couple of photos of the place. No vehicles were in sight, but I went ahead and walked to the front door and knocked. After waiting a few moments, I tried again. There was no answer and I couldn't hear anyone inside.

I returned to Carthage, where I tried to call Graham and the number for Conquest Labs. I left messages on an answering machine at CLI. The number I had been given for Graham turned out to be a wrong number. I tried again the next morning, once more leaving a message on the CLI answering machine, and working my sources in Lamar to find Graham's number. I had no luck. Despite dozens of attempts over the next two years, I was never able to talk to Graham for my stories, though I did later talk to a person or two who claimed to speak for him.

The court records also revealed part of the secret for Pat Graham's AIDS remission formula: It was going to be made from hogs' blood.

DIGGING INTO PAT GRAHAM'S BACKGROUND

As my stories about Pat Graham began running in the pages of *The Carthage Press*, one staff member was paying close attention, though I did not realize it at the time.

Finally one afternoon, photographer Ron Graber said, "There was man named Pat Graham who ripped off a lot of people in my home town. I think this is the same guy."

At that time, Ron had been at the Press for close to three years after graduating from the University of Missouri School of Journalism. His home town was Freeman, South Dakota., a town I had seen in one of the lawsuits that had been filed against Graham in Barton County Circuit Court. After that conversation, it did not take long for us to determine without a doubt that the Pat Graham who ripped off Conquest Labs investors was the same man who had fleeced the residents of Freeman, South Dakota.

"Is there anything I can do on this story?" Ron asked.

"Find some information on Graham's time in South Dakota," I responded and Ron went to work. It wasn't hog's blood that Graham was touting during his time in South Dakota, but fine dining.

Ron's investigation showed that on Oct. 26, 1977, Graham held a ground-breaking ceremony for The Cornerstone, a Christian-themed restaurant in Freeman. Plans for the restaurant included several private dining rooms, a picturesque fountain, and a stage for live gospel music. By the time of the restaurant's grand opening in September 1978, Graham had left Freeman, owing local tradesmen more than $130,000. First National Bank officials from whom Graham had borrowed money, filed a lawsuit claiming he owed them $173,766.31. A Denver, Colorado restaurant supply company sued for $90,271.83. Others filed suit, but most did not, fearing they would end up paying their lawyers more than they would ever receive from Graham. Freeman businessman Orville Waltner told Ron exactly what he thought of Graham. "Those kind, they'll do it once and if they crawl out they'll turn around and do it again. If Graham can beat this one, he'll just do it again. He doesn't care whose money he's doing it with."

As Ron worked on Graham's out-of—state shenanigans, I kept digging into court records. My search located a 1984 felony wire fraud conviction in U. S. District Court for the Western District of Missouri. Charges were filed against Graham after he offered to pay three southeast Kansas businessmen $25,000, which according to court records, he told them was "one half of my finder's fee from a gold sale in South Africa."

Court records indicated Graham already owed the three men $575,000. Pittsburg, Kansas insurance company owner August Rua was not surprised when I told him of Graham's activities. "Oh, yes, I remember Patrick Graham," Rua said. Rua, Ken DeLange, and Francis Usher, had been bilked out of their money, he said. When they became suspicious of Graham, Rua said, "We went to the FBI, and we filed charges against him."

Graham worked out a plea bargain agreement in which he would serve no prison time in exchange for his cooperation in other federal investigations. He was required to repay the $25,000. "We got back a little bit of money," Rua said, referring to the $25,000, but the rest of the money was lost forever."

◆   ◆   ◆

Patrick Graham's time in Missouri and his past in South Dakota were connected by one man, Dr. Duane Pankratz, owner of Grand Laboratories in Freeman, South Dakota. When Graham first came to Missouri, he attempted to establish a veterinary medicine business. In the lawsuits, Pankratz claimed Graham's business was based on Pankratz' patents. Pankratz began developing vaccines in the basement of his home in Ames, Iowa, in 1969, according to an article in the *Sioux Falls, S. D. Argus Leader*. His first product was an antiserum which prevented scours in piglets. From that base, he built Grand Laboratories, which during the mid-1990s was described as the fourth largest company of its type in the United States, with sales of approximately $15 million a year and with 71 items licensed by the U. S. Department of Agriculture. For a time in the 1970s and early 1980s, Pankratz had a partner—Pat Graham.

While Graham's Conquest Labs had no vaccine or serums to speak of, that was not the case with his first Lamar business, according to court records. When Graham moved from South Dakota to Missouri, he and Pankratz entered into an agreement which would allow Graham to sell the doctor's products in Missouri. Under the terms of the contract, Graham would pay Pankratz 50 cents per bottle.

In a lawsuit filed in Barton County Circuit Court, Pankratz claimed Graham breached the contract by cutting off the royalties. At a June 1979 stockholders meeting in Kansas City, Graham and his Missouri partners "issued themselves $40,000 worth of bonuses with Graham receiving $11,200," Pankratz claimed. The $40,000 was 30 percent of the company's earnings for the entire year.

Pankratz also claimed that he had loaned Graham $150,000 on July 21, 1977, to set up the Missouri business, with the condition that if he did not repay the loan, the business would be turned over to Pankratz. "The note is past due and Patrick D. Graham has not paid it nor complied with the other terms of the agreement," Pankratz said. A copy of the agreement was attached to the court file.

Pankratz won a $25,000 judgment against Graham in U. S. District Court on Nov. 5, 1982. Graham was also told to drop the name Grand Laboratories. In another lawsuit, Pankratz claimed Graham took the patents and used them at his second Lamar company, Mid-Continent Laboratories. The company was later purchased by Kansas City Southern Industries and in June 1992 a federal jury awarded Grand Laboratories and Pankratz $1.79 million in actual damages and $6.4 million in punitive damages for using trade secrets without paying for them. Of course, none of that hurt Pat Graham—by that time he was no longer with Mid-Continent Laboratories.

◆   ◆   ◆

As *The Carthage Press* continued its series of articles, word leaked that a grand jury had been impaneled in Barton County by Missouri Attorney General Jay Nixon, and that the panel's prime focus would be Pat Graham.

On the morning of Feb. 9, 1996, I received a fax from the attorney general's office saying that Nixon was holding a press conference at 1 p.m. that afternoon at the Joplin Airport. A few moments later, I received a call from someone in the attorney general's office asking if I had received the fax.

"Yes, it came about 15 minutes ago. Is this about Pat Graham?"

"I'm sorry. I can't give out any information about that." I hadn't expected her to tell me anything, but I had to take a shot. At that moment, I was facing the bane of any afternoon newspaper's existence—Ron and I had worked hard to keep on top of this story. In fact, we were the only ones covering it. The broadcast media shot footage of the raid on Conquest Labs, but had been absent after that. The *Joplin Globe* had published one story and the hometown *Lamar Democrat* had avoided the story entirely. Our deadline was 12 noon, and there was no way we could delay the printing for an out-of-town story.

We still had about two hours, so I made a few calls, coming up with nothing, then decided to write a speculative story in which I went with the only news we had, that the attorney general would be at the Joplin Airport for a 1 p.m. press conference … and then hedging my bets, that it could be an announcement of what was going to happen in the Pat Graham case. It wasn't much of a story, but it was the best we could do.

That afternoon, Ron and I arrived at the Joplin Airport about 15 minutes early and waited for the attorney general. We were escorted into a small room made even smaller by the entrance of reporters and cameras from the three local television stations, a Joplin Globe reporter, and Publisher Doug Davis of the *Lamar Democrat*.

After Nixon arrived, he quickly spelled out the indictment. Graham was being charged with 10 counts of fraud and 10 counts of selling unregistered securities. The attorney general's assistants handed out sheets laying out the entire case and I watched helplessly as every member of the area media now had the entire story handed to them after Ron Graber and I had been working on it for nine months. After Nixon spoke, he took questions. I didn't ask any. I was always a bit paranoid during press conferences. Normally, I just preferred not to allow the competition to benefit from the answers to my questions. In this case, however, I simply did not have any questions to ask.

It was a silent drive back to The Press as I assessed what we had. There was no doubt The Press had some background material the other media outlets did not have … but everyone had the main story. The electronic media would broadcast it nearly 20 hours before The Press hit the streets. The Globe would beat us by about 10 hours. We were going to be scooped on our own story.

I wrote the story, added some background info so at least our story would be more thorough, then the phone rang at my desk. It was a young lady from the attorney general's office.

"Mr. Turner, we wanted to make sure you had everything you needed."

"Yes, thank you." While I appreciated the follow-up call I was still feeling miserable about the lousy timing of the press conference.

We talked for a few more moments, then out of the blue, she said, "Wasn't that something about Pat Boone being one of the investors?"

I was no longer feeling sorry for myself. "Pat Boone was one of the investors?"

"His name was on the list." I almost jumped out of my seat.

"The Pat Boone, the singer?"

"Yes."

I tried to pry more information about the investor list from her, but she clearly had given me the information the attorney general (or more likely his public information officer) wanted me to have. It was one thing I always appreciated about Jay Nixon and Scott Holste. They knew which reporters were doing the work on which stories and they also knew the pitfalls of being a reporter on an afternoon newspaper.

I was back in the hunt. Though Pat Boone was no longer a superstar (and had not been for about four decades) at the time of Pat Graham's indictment, he was still well known. Boone had hit the top of the pop charts in the 1950s with such bland recordings as "Love Letters in the Sand," "Friendly Persuasion," "Don't Forbid Me," "Why Baby Why," and his vanilla covers of songs originated by African American artists, such as Little Richard's "Tutti Frutti" and Ivory Joe Hunter's "I Almost Lost My Mind." Boone had parlayed his musical success into the movies, most noticeably in the remake of the musical "State Fair," in 1962. After about an eight-year run on the pop charts, Boone stayed in the public eye for the next 30 years primarily as a guest on variety shows and through his commercials promoting milk.

Boone's clean-cut image brought him to Branson in the mid-1990s, where he attempted to follow the same path taken by other entertainers whose well of hits had long since dried up. He was exactly the type of person Pat Graham would target.

After about two hours of checking, I was able to come up with a number for the agency that represented Boone. My efforts to get through to the singer were unsuccessful and I never received a response in the months thereafter to a stream of phone calls and letters. Apparently, Pat Boone had no desire to talk to a reporter about his being taken for a ride by a rustic con man.

Nevertheless, I had my angle, the story that the *Joplin Globe*, the television stations, and the *Lamar Democrat* did not have. In the Feb. 10, 1996, Carthage Press, we revealed that Pat Boone was one of 105 investors who Pat Graham had bilked out of more than $5.3 million.

GRAHAM'S GUILTY PLEA
AND SENTENCING

In June 1997, in an effort to keep out of prison, Pat Graham offered to pay back the $5.3 million he had stolen from his investors. The offer was made by Graham's lawyer, C. R. Rhoades of Neosho, in a letter to Assistant Attorney General Douglas M. Ommen. Ommen was not impressed with the offer. "Obviously, I am very cynical about the ability of your client to raise $5.3 million in capital. He has personal liabilities in excess of $1 million, a prior plea of guilty to wire fraud, a prior corporate bankruptcy and no known proprietary interest or patent in any scientific products. I do not believe he is credit worthy for any funds without full security. I am deeply concerned about funds that he may be able to raise, as the very evidence in this case will prove that he defrauded investors."

In his letter to Rhoades, Ommen wrote, "Your client previously used this same tactic of 'imminent funding' in an effort to delay an action by the Barton County grand jury. Prior to that action, he claimed that funding was imminent. I can only hope this is not a ploy by your client to delay or avoid the trial by jury he faces next month."

Court records indicate Ommen offered Graham two alternative plea bargain agreements, which had been approved by the attorney general. Under the first, which involved no restitution, the 20 counts would be reduced to three. Graham would receive 10-year sentences on the first two counts to run concurrently, with a five-year sentence on the third count to run consecutively. The second plan would have also reduced the 20 counts to three, with Graham making full restitution. He would receive 10-year sentences on all three counts, but the third count would be suspended, and Graham would serve four months shock time in prison, and then could be released on probation if Circuit Court Judge David Darnold agreed. Graham was given a June 23, 1997 deadline; otherwise, his case would go to trial.

Graham agreed to the deal and wrote on the plea agreement document, "I knowingly sold securities on false representations and that had not been registered properly."

Graham admitted to telling investors that a public offering of Conquest Labs stock "would occur soon, when no such offering was coming. He said money would be used for development of an AIDS remission product, including the recruitment and hiring of scientists, when in fact, there was no such AIDS remission product and much of the money was used for the personal benefit of the defendant and various members of his family." Graham also admitted he did not tell his investors that he had been convicted of wire fraud in federal court in 1984.

The guilty plea was officially entered June 23, 1997. Sentencing was scheduled for September. Pat Graham had three months to figure out a way to stay out of prison.

◆   ◆   ◆

At the sentencing hearing, Judge Darnold made Graham a generous offer: "If someone wants to step up here and pay the $5.5 million," Darnold said, "I would be delighted.:

He had no takers.

But the game wasn't over yet. Pat Graham and his lawyer still had a few tricks up their sleeves, and it turned out to be one of the most entertaining court hearings I have ever attended.

The courtroom, on the second floor of the Barton County Courthouse, was packed. We had been the only media outlet to request having a still camera at the hearing and Judge Darnold did not place any major restrictions on Ron Graber, so he was able to get some good shots of Graham. I was seated on the front row, with my usual clipboard and yellow legal pad. I did not like the reporter notebooks, with the constant need to keep flipping through pages as you reached the bottom. The legal pad also gave me room for my usual practice, I always covered the meat of an event in the center of the page, writing my observations on the sides and in the corners.

The prosecution opened the hearing, calling three witnesses who had been taken in by Graham. It wasn't easy for the first one, Fred Staton, the former owner of the Lone Star Steakhouse in Branson, to admit he had been swindled. "I worked hard all my life." He sighed. "It's gone. My health's bad and I can't go out and start over."

Assistant Attorney General Doug Ommen asked, "How much money did you lose?"

"Three hundred fifty thousand dollars. It's embarrassing. I never invested in anything in my life other than CD bonds."

"Why did you invest in Conquest Labs?"

"I believed in Patrick Graham." Staton was followed by fellow investors Michael Zirbel, owner of Ozark Tour and Travel in Branson, and Ronald Blake.

Nancy Jones, a CPA working for the attorney general's office, said more than $1.3 million of investor money had been used for real estate, including $263,000 for a house for Graham and $236,900 for a house for Graham's daughter, Marcia Martinson, and her husband, Rod. Another $731,000 went directly to the Graham family, Ms. Jones said. "Very little money could be traced to anything remotely scientific in nature. Some money was used to pay off court judgments against Graham in Taney County, Missouri. Conquest Labs investor money was also used to buy presents for Graham's grandchildren."

The final prosecution witness was the man who supplied the information that led the government to Patrick Graham's doorstep—his son-in-law David Hoyt. Hoyt testified he had received a letter saying Conquest Labs might be breaking the law by selling too many unregistered securities within a 12-month period. When the sales continued to grow with no AIDS serum in sight, Hoyt said he became concerned and in September 1994 he called the secretary of state's office.. "I told them we had a problem and we needed help." After the secretary of state conducted the initial investigation, Graham signed a document saying he would sell no more securities, but it was to no avail.

"He kept on selling," Hoyt said, adding that the sales continued until May 22, 1995, when the Highway Patrol and Sheriff's Department raided Conquest Labs.

Three witnesses were called to show how Graham could pay back the investors. Robert E. Vance, a Henrietta, Oklahoma businessman, said, "I am involved in a very sensitive fund raising plan." He was working with a Carthage real estate investment group, he added. The group had a $30 million plan with the first $5.5 million earmarked to buy back the Conquest Labs shares.

With the rest of the money, Vance said, "we will form a business to market serum made of elk blood." Vance was somewhat taken aback when a steady stream of chuckles reverberated throughout the courtroom. Judge Darnold cast a stern look at the audience, looked as if he planned to bang his gavel, then he smiled and remained silent as the laughter faded.

Despite the reaction to his testimony, Vance continued without missing a beat. "My goal is to achieve enough money to pay all of his investors back. It is a waste of resource for that man," he said, pointing to Graham, "to be in prison. We would already have the money except for all of that hoopla in *The Carthage*

Press." Apparently, after some of the potential Carthage investors had learned about Graham, they backed out of the deal.

Vance proudly said, "I invested in Conquest Labs."

Judge Darnold did not appear to be impressed.

The second witness to support Graham was former Conquest Labs employee David Middleton, who insisted, "Work is being done on an AIDS serum." It didn't help Graham's case when, under cross-examination, Middleton admitted he had pleaded guilty to arson after setting his house on fire.

After Middleton left the stand, two more investors testified they did not want to see Graham behind bars. Retired Navy pilot Al Rusche, Billings, Missouri, who lost $40,000, said Graham was "certainly no threat to society" and it would be "an additional burden on the taxpayers and those of us who are investors if he is in prison and is not given an opportunity to pay back the money."

Cliff Braschler, owner of the Braschler Music Show of Branson, who lost $91,000, said, "Pat Graham did not ask me for money. I gave it freely. This does not warrant a 15-year sentence as far as I'm concerned."

After Braschler, Larry Bowen, an elk farmer, said he would be willing to hire Graham for his scientific expertise and would pay him at least $75,000 a year to help him develop and market serum from elks' blood.

That set the stage for the moment everyone was waiting for. Pat Graham was called to the stand. Graham quickly assured Judge Darnold the investors would be paid back.

"And how are you going to do this?" Darnold asked, leaning forward.

"I have an offer of a $10 million, 10-book deal with a Dallas publisher."

"You have a contract for this?" the judge asked.

"Well, no, not yet, but I have written two complete novels, I'm almost finished with a third novel and I have quite a bit remaining on the fourth." After a lengthy pause, Graham confided, "I have a Hollywood producer who is interested in one of my novels."

"Do you have a deal with this Hollywood producer?" the judge asked.

"No, but it's looking very promising."

"Do you have any other ideas for raising the money?"

Graham shook his head. "I am sorry for what I have done," he said. "I would like to not go to jail. I have a goal of paying back every one of my investors 100 percent. I would like to be with my family, my grandchildren and my church family and not be gone."

Darnold said he was not particularly impressed with either plan that had been offered. As for the elk blood serum plan, the judge said, he did not agree with the potential investors' faith in Graham. "You did not complete college, you took chemistry six times before getting a D grade. You received D's in algebra and trigonometry." Darnold was fair, however, and mentioned that there was one class in which Graham had excelled.

"I see you had a B in volleyball."

At that point, Graham's shoulders slumped. It was obvious where this was going. As for the book deal, Judge Darnold said, "People write books every day and say someone in Hollywood is going to produce them.

"I don't believe the Conquest Labs investors are ever going to get their money back." As Darnold sentenced Graham to 15 years in prison, he offered him one ray of hope. If he could find a way to pay back the investors by the time his first four months in prison had been completed, he might be freed.

The investors lost all of their money.

Pat Graham was a defeated man, as he was escorted out of the courtroom. As I wrote a few final notes, I failed to see a young couple in their 30s approaching me. "Are you Randy Turner?" the man asked.

"Yes."

For the first time, I met Pat Graham's daughter, Michelle Hoyt, and son-in-law, David Hoyt. Michelle Hoyt's eyes were reddened.

"We never wanted it to come to this," David Hoyt said. "I felt we had a responsibility to those investors. Those people were being cheated."

"People think we took that money," Michelle Hoyt said, "but we didn't come out of this with a cent. I want people to know that."

We talked for a few more moments and I watched them as they left the Barton County Courthouse. I couldn't even imagine what that family was going through. At that point, I imagined Pat Graham would spend three or four years behind bars and then be released. Once he entered the prison system, however, Pat Graham never saw daylight again.

For the next 10 years, Graham filed one motion after another, all unsuccessful efforts to have his sentence overturned. In his first appeal, he claimed Judge Darnold was prejudiced against him and had told Barton County Sheriff Bill Griffitt, Circuit Clerk Jerry Moyer and assistant attorneys general Ommen and Sue Sperry he was "finally going to put that (expletive) where he belongs." Graham never said who told him that; it didn't make any difference, no one was buying into the story. He exhausted his appeals in Barton County and in state courts, then tried his best to have his sentence overturned in federal court. Nothing worked.

In April 2007, a *Turner Report* reader e-mailed me, telling me she had heard Pat Graham had died in prison. A quick check of the state prisoner status website confirmed his death. In the April 12, 2007, *Turner Report*, I wrote about Graham, once again telling the Conquest Labs story. I was shocked by the response from a handful of readers.

One wrote: "Patrick Graham was past due for release. Those who murder serve less time. Those who murdered this man shall pay. Try reporting the truth-IF you are smart enough to figure out what that is."

Another said, "As a close, personal friend of the late Pat Graham and his family, I feel it important to point out some…. "misinformation" that was in this piece.

"First, never once, EVER, did I hear Pat or anyone from Conquest claim they HAD a cure for aids. It was stated many times that they were WORK-ING on a cure. I feel that there is a difference.

"Second: Why do you mock the faith and religion of a dead man? Everything I know of Patrick Graham was of Lord God and Jesus Christ. His belief in Christ and the belief that He was savior was ALWAYS real and passionate. Is it really such a stretch of the mind to think that someone who makes a mistake could also have an unmovable faith in God?

"Last, I would just like to say, that I AM NOT saying and never will say that what happened with Conquest Labs was right or acceptable. It was wrong to misuse the investors' money. However, I know (as well as anyone else that knew Pat), that it wasn't intentional. What happened was the same thing that would likely happen to most of us in that situation. It started with "a little here, and I'll pay it right back" and snowballed from there.

I don't know if you have a personal vendetta, or just never liked the situation, but please, for the sake of his family and friends, stop beating a dead horse … so to speak."

The same man later wrote, "My question to you still remains: is this a personal vendetta or just "objective" reporting?

"As for that being the way he is remembered, it is obvious that you either didn't know him or you do, in fact, have something personal against him. I would be very interested what this thing is.

"Should we all be judged for 1 or 2 actions in our lives? Should our loved ones be forced to bear our sins when we're gone from this world?

"Or, is it possible to be judged for our life as a WHOLE? Is it too much to ask that those close to me not have to pay my way when I'm dead and gone? Can I not be judged for the things I did that were good and have the bad be forgiven?

Is it too much to ask to NOT be judged in death? In life? At all?"

Another Graham supporter offered this comment:

"As a former member of the company that had worked with many of the people involved with the 'vaccine', I can only ask myself, "Why?" Why did you report wrong information? Why did you feel it is important for your ego to report that he was "bilking" money from just "Branson royalty". There were many other fine individuals that assisted to create and support this company. All did lose their money. Yes, they paid the price for greed. Yet you blame only one individual for it, because it was his company. Yes, there was the research of many medications being developed, but you chose to only write about one and how it was false. So I take it, you personally knew then. Patrick was a great man, a kind and gentle man, he would give his shirt to any soul if needed. I could not have had a better person to have known. He cared about people and friends and family. He poured his heart into what he believed was right.

Trying to understand why the state of Missouri made it clear that he would not leave prison alive, I guess they were right. It saddens me beyond to think that for spending money not intended allows reporters and government officials to punish and keep punishing him, it doesn't make sense to me. They gave him parole, but kept him prisoner. I don't understand why people from other states contribute financial support for our Missouri officials, whoops, by accident they were also those involved in this case, strange if you ask me. Pat paid for what he did in more ways than just printed in black and white. He paid the price of never seeing his grandchildren grow up, graduate or even hold his great-grandchildren. He missed every graduation; one would have been next month, two of which passed several years ago. I can't compare of what he did to any other white collar crime, but the man took his medicine and you celebrate his death and rub it in his family's face. Do you think maybe you could have some compassion for them? They also had to deal with loss. I am no longer associated with his family and I pray that one day AIDS will be cured. How can you appreciate the loss? You write odd! He did not obtain 5 million dollars by fraud, you make it sound as though he spent every penny on himself and his family, wrong again, you only have bits and pieces of truth and that makes you full of bunk. I wish you had spoke with me, then you might have really known the truth, but you are afraid of the truth. You remain to hide behind your black and white written trash, yes it supports you because people of all walks of life like to read, mostly half truths and trash. As for me I will remember Patrick D. Graham as a faithful Christian man who I can say was my best friend and mentor. You knew nothing of him and that is sad! I will forever miss him, may he finally rest in peace."

I will echo that final sentiment.

THE TURNPIKE KILLER

When you work for a small-town newspaper, even if you are the editor, there are certain events you have to cover. I was never big on Chamber of Commerce dinners. The people who attended them were nice people, no doubt, but I was never comfortable.

In early 1998, a few months after Ralph Bush became publisher of *The Carthage Press*, he, Ron Graber and I attended the annual Carthage Chamber of Commerce Banquet at the Precious Moments Convention Center.

For me, it was bad enough to be at a job where I was required to wear a tie everyday. Since the Chamber dinner was a big deal, I had to wear a suit, so I was feeling out of place right from the start.

Before the banquet began, during the social part of the evening, one Carthage bigwig after another kept coming up and talking to Ron Graber, who was always good in these situations. Meanwhile, nearly every person who was waiting on the tables and working in the back, came up and talked to me. It was one of the few things that made the evening bearable.

Banquets, receptions, social functions, none of these were ever my cup of tea, but I never felt that way about some of the events that I covered that other reporters avoided like the plague. While our sports editors were always big on covering high school varsity sports, I never minded attending junior varsity sports or junior high sports. I never minded beauty pageants, and I could always get a good feature out of a baby show.

One such show took place in August 1993 at the Jasper United Methodist Church, the annual Jasper Appreciation Days Baby Show. When you have covered baby shows for nearly two decades, you know there is one question that brings an automatic response ... and it is the same one every time.

When did you first know you had a prize-winning baby?

The answer, of course—"I knew it the minute he (or she) was born," or words that are remarkably similar. Sheila Mayfield felt the same way about her youngest son, Clayton, an entrant in the Appreciation Days contest.

When I walked into the church, I looked around to see if there was anyone I recognized. I knew Sheila Mayfield, formerly Gordon, from her days at Jasper

High School. I had covered activities involving Sheila and her younger sister, Shelly, when I was at the *Lamar Democrat.*. She and Clayton were sitting alone in a back pew, so I slid in beside them and renewed our friendship. Fortunately, for my baby show story, though it was quite by coincidence, I had also latched onto the winning baby and his mother.

"Is that a prize winning baby?" I asked, already preparing for the questions I would have to ask the mother of the winning infant after the show ended.

"Of course," Sheila said, a big smile never leaving her face.

A few moments later, it was time for her category, 0-3 month-old boys. The mothers stood in the front of the room as three judges, two women and a man, went down the line, making remarks about each baby, and watching intently as mothers tried to calm crying babies, rocking them, bouncing up and down, making the kinds of silly noises adults always use to entertain babies. Sheila did not have to resort to any of those tactics. Clayton just rested in his mother's arms, smiling and occasionally waving his arms in delight. The judges were captivated.

Clayton received first prize in his category, but that did not mean his part in the show, or Sheila's, was anywhere near over. As a first-prize winner, Clayton was now eligible for the grand prize. Sheila and Clayton slipped into an adjoining room, and Clayton's pleasant disposition vanished, as he began growing a bit fussy. "He just hasn't had a nap," Sheila said. She gave him his bottle, but that did not work. She took him into the church's nursery where after several anxious moments, he finally fell into a deep sleep, just the antidote for a cranky baby.

When it was time for all of the winners to parade in front of the judges for the grand prize, Sheila had to wake her son. It was a moment she dreaded. "I didn't know what he was going to be like when he woke up," she said.

She didn't have to worry. Clayton Mayfield was an angel and for a second time, he charmed the judges and walked away with the grand championship prize. Photo after photo was taken of the champion baby and his mother. I managed to get a good one, though I am sure it was the same shot all of the other photographers landed. While Clayton was looking at the camera, a bit curious about all of the attention he was receiving, his mother never looked at any of the photographers, except during one photo when she was asked to look up. Her loving gaze was reserved for Clayton, who rested in her right arm, while she carried his grand prize trophy in her left hand. It would not have mattered a bit to Sheila if Clayton had not won the contest … she already had her prize. The trophy and the attention for her son, that was just the icing on the cake.

Sheila Mayfield had the champion baby, but as she was quick to tell me, it was just one of her champion babies. "I have another one at home."

Fourteen years have passed since the 1993 Jasper Appreciation Days Baby Show, but that picture of Sheila Mayfield smiling and adoringly gazing at her prize-winning son Clayton is as fresh in my mind now as it was then.

It was the last time I ever saw Sheila.

◆   ◆   ◆

Sheila Mayfield was a working mother, first at Southwest Missouri Bank in Carthage, and later at the bank's Jasper branch, but the desire to spend as much time with her family as possible led her to leave the job in late 1993.

"It was a hard decision for her to make," her former boss Elaine Joines told me. "She agonized over it, but the most important thing to her was her family and she wanted to be home with her children."

In addition to her two children and her husband, Ben Mayfield, Sheila cared for an elderly couple who lived nearby, cooking for them and taking her kids over to see them and brighten their day.

In January 1994, she learned she was going to have the opportunity to teach the Mission Friends Sunday school class at her church on Jan. 12, 1994. She was excited about it, but it never happened. The day before her new duties were to begin, Sheila Mayfield was murdered. Ben Mayfield became a widower, and Ryan and Clayton Mayfield had to grow up without a mother.

Sheila, her sister, Shelly Wells, and her grandmother, Velta Ball, were returning from a Miami, Oklahoma hospital where Sheila and Shelly's mother, Peggy Gordon, was recovering from surgery. They were less than one mile from the Missouri state line when a rock was thrown from an overpass on the Will Rogers Turnpike, crashing through the windshield and killing Sheila instantly. Sheila's grandmother was able to reach over, grab the steering wheel and bring the car to a stop, preventing further tragedy. Sheila Mayfield was only 25 years old.

It wasn't long before two teenage boys were arrested for the murder. One, 15-year-old Benji Trammel, pleaded guilty, was sent to a juvenile correctional facility, was released when he turned 18 and now has a clean record.

The other, Paul Murray, was 16 years old and because of that extra year was tried as an adult. During his preliminary hearing, Ottawa County, Oklahoma Undersheriff (now Sheriff) Terry Durborow testified that when Murray and Trammel were arrested at Quapaw High School "they didn't act like they were too worried."

Though Trammel's case was decided quickly, it was a long road to justice where the other killer, Paul Wesley Murray, was concerned.

More than five years passed before Murray finally pleaded guilty to murder in the second degree. He was initially charged with first degree murder after Oklahoma officers found a notebook in his school locker which depicted the same scenario which had claimed Sheila Mayfield's life—a chilling drawing of someone throwing a rock from an overpass and killing someone that had been drawn before the rock was thrown at Sheila Mayfield's car.

Later, the charge against Murray was downgraded to second degree murder, to get Murray to enter his plea and to finally bring the case to a close. Even then, it couldn't have brought much satisfaction to Sheila's family. Murray entered an Alford plea, meaning he conceded there was enough evidence to convict him, but he was not saying he was actually guilty.

During the five years between Sheila Mayfield's death and Paul Murray's sentencing, Murray had married and the couple had a boy, both of whom were in the courtroom to support Murray.

Peggy Gordon watched as her daughter's killer was sentenced. "It's been five years and we're ready to put it all behind us," she told John Hacker, who was covering the sentencing for The Press.

Mrs. Gordon watched as Murray was brought into the courtroom in handcuffs, with his wife, son and mother behind him. "Nobody wanted it to come to this. He has a little boy and a wife, so nobody wins."

As part of the plea agreement, as *The Carthage Press* reported in Hacker's story in the Feb. 2, 1999, issue, Murray's sentence was to be reviewed in 120 days and if he maintained good behavior during that time, his sentence would be reduced from 15 to only five years in prison.

I never had the chance to follow up on what happened to Paul Murray after those 120 days. By the time June 1999 rolled around, neither John Hacker nor I were on the Press staff. John was working elsewhere, and I was on the unemployment line, still two months away from becoming a middle school English teacher … and Paul Murray was walking the streets again. No five-year sentence, just the four months. This despite the fact that at the same time he was pleading no contest to the murder charge, Murray had pleaded guilty to a misdemeanor marijuana charge and to driving while intoxicated.

Murray was released after four months despite a pre-sentence investigation which said he remained a "danger and a threat to the community and himself."

If the death of Sheila Mayfield had not taken place, and he had not been arrested, Murray told those who conducted the pre-sentence investigation, "I might have done something really bad."

As of mid-summer 1999, Paul Murray was a free man. His brushes with the law did not end. On March 12, 2002, he pleaded guilty to a public intoxication charge. Four months later, he was stopped and charged with not wearing a seat belt. On March 10, 2003, it was failure to pay child support.

Finally, and no information is available from court records as to what ended up sending Murray to prison, it was determined that he had violated the terms of his parole and he was sent to the Oklahoma State Reformatory in Granite on Sept. 11, 2003.

For killing Sheila Mayfield, Paul Murray eventually spent about four years in prison. He was released on July 4, 2007 and will remain on probation through May 7, 2013.

Both of Sheila Mayfield's killers are free men.

A few months ago, as I was leaving my dentist's office in Lamar, I saw Sheila's mother, Peggy Gordon, in the parking lot. We talked about Clayton and Ryan and Shelly. Life goes on, and for the Gordons, Sheila lives through their memories and through those two boys.

I hope Ryan Mayfield, who is 14 as I write this, has had a chance to look at those pictures showing him and his mother at the Jasper Appreciation Days Baby Show. Those pictures show two winners ... and a love that even the senseless violence of two teenage brutes can never erase.

THE DAY OF THE LIVING DEAD

The first and only time I raised the dead was a little over 23 years ago.

I was editor of the *Lamar Democrat* in the early 1980s when we ran an obituary on a former presidential candidate who died at a young age.

I was still the Democrat's editor a year later, when I saw that same man, Lamar native James R. Montgomery, walking into a bar, as it turned out it was the same bar in which Montgomery had written his own obituary and announced his untimely demise.

My first meeting with Montgomery came when I was editor of the *Lockwood Luminary-Golden City Herald* in May 1979. A woman called me that morning at the Lockwood office to tell me about a press conference which was going to be held in Lamar that afternoon in which Montgomery, who was living in Oronogo, Missouri, at the time, planned to announce he was a candidate for president of the United States. I asked who James R. Montgomery was and though I did not receive a satisfactory answer, since I was going to be in Lamar anyway, I decided to cover the event.

The announcement was supposed to take place at the bandstand on the Lamar square. I arrived about 10 minutes early to scope out the site and saw a tall, silver-haired gentleman standing by the courthouse steps, surrounded by photographers and reporters from KOAM, and KTVJ (later KSNF) and Lou Nell Clark from the *Lamar Democrat*, the woman who gave me my shot in journalism when she hired me to be sports editor at the Democrat in May 1978 after my disastrous nine-month stint as editor and advertising salesman for the *Newton County News*.

The cameras were trained on the silver-haired gentleman as he began speaking, and when he spoke, the words flowed, just like the image of a southern politician from hundreds of old movies. You could almost see the honey dripping from his mouth.

Lou Nell, as always, was taking notes furiously, adding row after row of the politician's comments. Meanwhile, I walked over to the bandstand where a smaller, balding gentleman, almost a dead ringer for the late actor Wally Cox, was standing, staring at a notebook in his hand and talking to himself.

I approached him and played a hunch. "Mister Montgomery?" I asked.

"Yes," he answered in a high-pitched, girlish voice.

I introduced myself, and while Lou Nell and the television reporters were interviewing Montgomery's vice presidential candidate, Leo Suiter, I had an exclusive with the presidential candidate. It would have been great if he had actually had anything worthwhile to say.

It was Suiter who served as the mouthpiece for his running mate. The official speech began a few moments later, when Suiter spoke of his love for Missouri. "If I'm not in heaven, then I'm in the closest thing to it." Then he went into attack mode. "Our lives are being controlled by the one-world socialist government conspiracy." I looked around for all of the people who were ready to jump on the Montgomery-Suiter bandwagon, but someone must have given them the wrong time.

"Our problems," Suiter said, "can be blamed on two things—the Federal Reserve system and the graduated income tax." Suiter then enlightened the audience with a recitation of the history of the one-world government conspiracy. "Their goal is to strip all nations of their sovereignty and bring the world under one socialist government.

"These people are everywhere, President Jimmy Carter, Richard Nixon, David Eisenhower, George Bush (who was a candidate for president at that time and would become vice president) U. N. Ambassador Andrew Young, Shirley Temple Black, Vice President Walter Mondale and the president of Coca-Cola.

"Is it any wonder that the people of Coca-Cola knew about the normalization of relations with China before the Congress?"

Suiter accused President Carter of "giving away the Panama Canal," but said all is not lost. "If President Carter can give it away, James R. Montgomery can get it back when he is elected in 1980."

The spectacle was heightened when Suiter, playing on the comedy of errors that President Carter's hard-drinking brother Billy brought to the White House in the late 1970s, introduced his own brother Billy, who was dressed in overalls, smoked a pipe and claimed he was looking for something to drink, but could only find a Mountain Dew.

Montgomery and Suiter were swallowed up in the 1980 presidential race; in fact, I never heard anything from either of them before Ronald Reagan was elected in November 1980. It was well documented in early 1980 when President Carter, talking about the possibility of a challenge from Massachusetts Senator

Ted Kennedy, said, "If Ted Kennedy runs, I'll whip his ass." No one ever reported on the rumor that Carter also said, "And that goes for James R. Montgomery, too." After all, Suiter had said that he and Montgomery had considered running for the Democratic nomination, but had decided Carter had it locked up.

The story of how Montgomery and Suiter got together was a fascinating one. Suiter saw an ad Montgomery had placed in *Country Music* magazine looking for a vice presidential candidate. (Some say Dan Quayle was chosen in the same manner.)

After the 1980 presidential election, it appeared that the media would not have James R. Montgomery to kick around any more, and then it appeared his career had come to a tragic end when he died at age 42 in 1982.

You can say all you want about Richard Nixon's political comeback. All he did was lose a 1962 race for governor of California to Pat Brown, then bounced back and was elected president six years later.

James R. Montgomery came back from the dead in 1983. I asked him about his "death," and he leaned forward and spoke in a near whisper.

"I wasn't really dead."

I wrote down every word he spoke for the historical record. "My enemies were the ones who said I was dead," he confided.

"You have enemies?"

"Oh, dear me, yes," he said, the weight on the world weighing on his slumping shoulders.

"Who are these enemies?"

"The socialists."

"The socialists?" Then I remembered. "You talked about them when you were running for president." Actually, it was Leo Suiter who talked about them, but what difference did it make?

Montgomery nodded. "They were the ones who kept me from being president?"

Damned socialists!

"And they put your obituary in the *Joplin Globe*?"

"Yes, and the *Carthage Press* and in your newspaper." I was back at the *Lamar Democrat* by that time.

"Why would they do this?"

"They were afraid of what I could do."

So was I. Happy that he was still alive, despite the efforts of those dastardly socialists, I waited for James R. Montgomery to mount his political comeback. It happened in 1987.

Not content to run for one office, Montgomery filed for two. He set his sights considerably lower than president of the United States. He filed for Ward One alderman on the Lamar City Council and for a seat on the Barton County Health Department Board of Trustees.

And apparently, he was at the top of his game. Not one socialist challenged him. But others stood in James R. Montgomery's way.

SEARCHING FOR A MONTGOMERY WARD

The entry of James R. Montgomery into the Ward One Lamar City Council race made it a three-way battle. With no incumbent running, all Montgomery, a veteran of a national presidential race, had to do was to beat two rookies, Max Simmons, who had no idea of what he was getting into, and *Lamar Democrat* Publisher Doug Davis.

Always an astute politician, Montgomery put himself on the side of the angels. "This is one poor person, me, against the Lamar rich," he told me, as he staked his claim for the vote of the little guy. And he must have been involved in politics for a long time. On a candidate questionnaire he filled out for the Democrat, Montgomery, 46 at the time, claimed he had "46 years of experience in government."

The veteran campaigner had no fear of launching a broadside against the most powerful company in Lamar, O'Sullivan Industries. "Right now, we have only one large manufacturer that seems to monopolize the labor force. When a company monopolizes, you leave the door open for discrimination."

Montgomery also claimed he would clean out the "lazy city employees. We have too many just putting in their time while those who do the work get little wages. The ones making the high salaries just sit around and goof off all day long."

He vowed to work for those who were victims of discrimination. "I know what discrimination is. I've been there."

Montgomery's chances for election were improved when one of his opponents, Davis, discovered that Missouri conflict-of-interest laws might keep his newspaper from being able to accept any advertising from the city if he were elected. Davis said that a law that would require the city to seek competitive bids each time it needed to put a legal notice in the *Lamar Democrat* would cause considerable problems for him and for the city. If the city had to take bids, Davis said, it would have to publish a legal notice saying it was taking bids on the advertisement and would have no place in which to do it.

"This law is absurd," Davis said, and he blamed political activist Lou Rix, who had been unsuccessful in an effort to unseat longtime Lamar Mayor Gerald Gilkey, but who had been successful in her efforts to open Lamar city government to the citizens. Davis said Mrs. Rix would have used the law against him if he were elected.

"If it hadn't been for her, I could have served the city. I don't think anyone else would have been bothered by it."

Mrs. Rix said she didn't think that was true. "I did not have anything to do with the law when it was written years ago, but I agree with it 100 percent. Besides, I wonder what other laws he is obeying just because I live in Lamar."

Davis dropped out of the race, making the announcement in the Democrat that he would not be able to serve if elected.

Only Max Simmons, an employee of O'Sullivan Industries, stood between James R. Montgomery and political power.

A few days later, in my capacity as *Lamar Democrat* editor, I served as a moderator of a candidate forum in the Lamar Middle School cafeteria. The forum included the mayoral candidates, incumbent Gerald Gilkey and challenger Dr. Kent Torbeck, Third Ward candidates Marion Elswick, the incumbent, and Pat Ross, and Simmons and Montgomery from the First Ward.

Montgomery was a no-show, and though Davis' departure from the race, had put him in a good position, Montgomery's own candidate questionnaire had put his candidacy in jeopardy.

Montgomery claimed to be a member of the Screen Actors Guild, the American Federation of Radio and Television Artists (AFTRA) and the American Society of Composers and Publishers (ASCAP).

I checked with officials from those organizations and they had no record of a James R. Montgomery ever having been a member.

He also claimed to be a member of three non-existent organizations, Christians United for Justice, Americans Against Political Punishment, and Christians Against Drunk Doctors. He even said he had served on the board of directors of Christians Against Drunk Doctors. (And wouldn't the world be a better place if such an organization existed?)

An apparently fake charity drive in 1986 also came back to haunt Montgomery. The *Joplin Globe* reported that Lamar area churches and the Boy Scouts were helping Montgomery with a door-to-door canned food drive. I checked with the Lamar Police Department and with the Barton County Division of Family Services. Police Chief Ron Hager told me Montgomery had broken no laws but his activities were "questionable."

Montgomery, always the glib politician, told me had been misquoted by the Globe. "I didn't say the Boy Scouts would be helping, I said some Boy Scouts would.

"They also misquoted me about the churches," he insisted. "I didn't say churches would be helping us, just some church members."

The drive never took place.

With Davis out of the race and Montgomery crippled by these revelations, Max Simmons emerged as the front runner.

So that was the political atmosphere on March 23, 1987, as the candidate forum began. It was the strangest, and most memorable, candidate forum I have ever attended, much less served as moderator. It started with the mayor's debate when the challenger, Dr. Torbeck, claimed he was the best looking candidate. Mayor Gilkey's wife Betty, jumped to her feet. "That is not true," she said, as nearly everyone in the cafeteria laughed.

Then when it was time for the Ward One candidates to be announced, only Simmons was on the stage. It did not stay that way for long. Doug Davis entered from the hallway and strode purposefully to the stage and announced what he had already put in the newspaper, he was not able to run. After a few remarks, he left the stage and the cafeteria.

Since Montgomery was not there, Max Simmons had the stage to himself. "My job's getting easier," he said. "I found out this morning one of my opponents has dropped out. I don't know my opponent James Montgomery. I appreciate your vote and I'll do my best for my ward and the entire city."

Montgomery later told me he was not able to appear at the forum because he was in Kansas City attending a civil rights seminar.

The next stunning development in the First Ward race occurred right after the forum when Davis changed his mind and decided to re-enter the race, running full-page advertisements in the Democrat, declaring "I can serve."

When the ballots were cast, Doug Davis was elected First Ward alderman with 242 votes, followed by Simmons with 162 and Montgomery with 16.

But lest we forget, Montgomery was running for two positions in that April election and he had far more success in his other race. The incumbent in the Barton County Health Department race was Lou Rix and she had ruffled the feathers of many of the leading politicians in the city, who decided it would be amusing to push Montgomery's candidacy. They pushed it so well, he ended up with 1,409 votes. It was a four-way race for three positions and Mrs. Rix barely edged Montgomery for the third spot.

After his double defeat, times grew tough for the one-time presidential contender. In September 1988, the *Joplin Globe* reported that Montgomery was living in a cardboard box on the banks of Muddy Creek. Montgomery told the newspaper his trailer house had burned on May 12, 1988, and he had been left homeless and had slept in the box, which he described as "like sleeping in your own grave."

Having considerable experience with James R. Montgomery, I checked the story and was told by a Golden City resident that during much of the time Montgomery was allegedly sleeping in a cardboard box, he was staying at a home in Golden City.

After the Globe story was printed, Barton County law enforcement officials found no evidence that anyone had been living on the banks of Muddy Creek. In March 1989, James R. Montgomery, under a plea bargain agreement, pleaded guilty in Barton County Circuit Court to a charge of misdemeanor stealing. He admitted to changing a $5 Salvation Army voucher to $55 and trying to pass it off at Lamar Supermarket. Judge David Darnold followed Prosecuting Attorney James Nichols' recommendation and sentenced Montgomery to 60 days in the Barton County Jail, and then placed him on supervised probation for one year.

After this fall from grace, it appeared the storied political career of James R. Montgomery had come to a close, but he bounced back for one more campaign. In 1991, Montgomery, 50 at the time, ran once again for the Health Department Board of Trustees. Even with no anti-Rix campaign to boost his total, he still managed to garner 677 votes to finish fourth once again in a three-way race. Defeating him were incumbents Larry Kuhn with 2,070 votes, Doris Kelsey with 1,987, and Karen Wegener with 1,832.

Eventually Montgomery left Barton County. While current Lamar High School journalism teacher Holly Sundy Willhite, who worked for me at the Democrat from 1987 to 1990, was attending Southwest Missouri State University (now Missouri State University), she saw Montgomery in Springfield pushing his latest business venture.

Since that time, I have lost track of James R. Montgomery. At one time, I heard he was in dire need of a kidney transplant. Later, I heard that he had died. I was never able to track down the truth.

In the back of my mind I keep hoping that Montgomery made up this latest death story in another bar and that he will return and make another run for political office. In this era, a man with his credentials could probably run for president and be invited to the never-ending debates.

At other times, I think about what could have happened. Doug Davis was on the Lamar City Council for more than a decade, but if he had stayed out of that race and if Montgomery had not made his critical mistakes, who knows? He might have been elected Ward One alderman.

Lamar could have had a Montgomery Ward.

TWO DRUNKS IN A MOTEL ROOM

I have always prided myself on my news judgment, but there was one time when it failed me completely.

On the morning of April 19, 1995, Publisher Jim Farley, back from his morning trip to the Carthage Police Department headquarters and coffee with Chief Ed Ellefsen, popped his head into the newsroom and said there was a major story, an explosion at a federal building in Oklahoma City. What my problem was, I cannot tell you, but it didn't click me with me for some time that morning, that this was a major story. At first, before I saw the stories coming over the Associated Press wire, I did not realize that this was deliberately set, an act of homegrown terrorism. *The Carthage Press* did give the story the full page-one treatment it deserved, but as Jim reminded me for the rest of the time we worked together, my judgment on that story was lacking.

I made up for that lack of judgment less than two weeks later when the Oklahoma City bombing story made its way to Carthage.

◆　　　◆　　　◆

It was mid-afternoon May 1 when two men in a white Thunderbird with Arizona license plates wheeled into the Kel-Lake Motel parking lot, jumped out of the car and headed to the motel office.

One of the men was in his 50s, a tall, slender gentleman wearing a dark red cap and a blue flannel shirt. The other man, was in his late 20s, and had a stocky build, long black hair and a thin mustache. He wore a dark blue polo shirt.

The men were smiling as they entered the office. Wanda Jackson, who owned the motel with her husband Norman, greeted them.

"We're looking for a room," the older man said.

"We have some rooms."

"Great. We would like to pay for a week," the older man said, "but we would like to see the room first." The men introduced themselves. The older man was Robert Jacks, while the younger one was Gary Allen Land.

"Do you have cable?" Land asked.

Assured that the rooms had cable, Land asked, "How about HBO?"

"Yes, we have HBO?"

Land nodded.

As Mrs. Jackson led the men to a room on the far end of the property, she struck up a conversation with the men. "What brings you to Missouri?" she asked.

"We're looking to stay somewhere for a spell," Jacks said. "We're hoping to buy a place somewhere around here."

As they approached the room, the men were surprised to see ducks and geese strolling through the property as if they owned it.

"Do you have those all the time?" Jacks asked.

"They come over from Kellogg Lake," Mrs. Jackson explained.

She turned the key and opened the room, a plain-looking room with two beds and a television. After they looked over the room for a couple of moments, they agreed to take it, returned with Mrs. Jackson, signed the register and paid for a week's stay.

A few moments later, the two jumped into the Thunderbird and drove off, returning about a half hour later with large boxes from Pizza Hut and what appeared to be enough beer to get them through the evening and maybe a few more evenings.

The next morning well before dawn, motel owner Norman Jackson glanced at the register and saw the names. "Gary Allen Land, Robert Jacks," he said aloud, and the names were immediately familiar to them. He told his wife, "These are the guys on CNN. These are the ones they are looking for about the Oklahoma City bombing." The CNN report had not only included the names of Land and Jacks, but had also given a description and license number of the white Thunderbird with Arizona license plates, the same car that was parked in front of the motel.

Seeing a Missouri Highway Patrol car in the parking lot of the Flying W convenience store across the street, Jackson, taking extra care not to look like he was doing anything out of the ordinary, walked across the street and approached the trooper.

"I think the guys at the motel are the ones the FBI is looking for in the Oklahoma City bombing," he said.

"What makes you think that?" the trooper asked.

After Jackson described the car and the names the men had written on the register, the trooper was convinced. The trooper checked the car, which was registered to Land. Two men in that same car had checked into a Vinita, Oklahoma motel the afternoon of the bombing, left the next morning, and returned later in the afternoon.

After the trooper called in, it was not long before state, federal, city and county law enforcement were in the area, using the Flying W as a command post. The moment, the FBI arrived, it took charge and agents quietly went to the rooms of other guests to evacuate them and protect them in case anything went wrong with the arrest of Land and Jacks.

The agents did not rush making sure everyone was set up in their proper places before they even started the orderly evacuation of the other motel guests.

George and Jacque Williams were sound asleep when two FBI agents knocked on their door at about 5:30 a.m. A groggy George Williams answered the door. The agents flashed their badges and said, "You need to leave this room as quickly as possible."

"What's going on?" George Williams asked.

"I'm afraid we can't tell you that, but you have to leave and you need to leave quietly."

Williams said he would and in a few moments, he and his wife were on their way. One more guest was moved out of his room before the FBI contacted Land and Jacks.

An agent called the motel room, where the men, surrounded by empty Bigfoot Pizza Hut boxes and beer cans that were just as empty, were wide awake, watching movies on HBO.

"You need to come out of the room with your hands over your heads," the FBI agent said to Land, who had answered the phone. "Don't make any sudden moves."

More than 50 Missouri Highway Patrol troopers and federal agents were blanketing the Kel-Lake Motel parking lot, aiming weapons at the motel room from every angle. It was a few moments before the door opened, and Land and Jacks exited the room, their hands over their heads.

FBI agents patted them down, handcuffed them, put them in a burgundy patrol car, and they were back on their way to Carthage.

♦　　　♦　　　♦

Though *Carthage Press* Publisher Jim Farley did not write any stories for The Press, he served up a consistent flow of scoops for his reporters, from the police department and from other sources in government and business during the seven years I worked with him.

On the morning of May 2, 1995, Farley called me at home. He had received a tip that suspects in the Oklahoma City bombing were being arrested.

"You're kidding?"

"No, I'm not kidding. This is on the level," he said.

I told him I would be right there. I was already almost out the door anyway and I only lived about six blocks from The Press. Shortly after I arrived, Ron Graber, the staff photographer, entered the office. I explained the situation and told him to be ready. We were going to offer comprehensive coverage of this story. For once, we would have the advantage over the morning newspaper. A few moments later, Lifestyles Editor Mary Guccione, a former *Joplin Globe* reporter who had worked for the Press for about two months, came in. Mary was an ambitious reporter who always tried to work her way into big stories, even though those did not always come with her job description. I told her she was going to play a big part in this one.

That left me with one more person to call. "I need to call Kaiser," I said, referring to our police reporter Randee Kaiser (now a Carthage policeman)."

"You can't call him," Mary said. "He's on vacation."

"If I don't call him, he's never going to forgive me. He'll want to be in on this one."

When I called, his wife answered the phone and it appeared Randee was having a heck of a vacation. "He's fixing the roof," his wife said. She finally agreed to let me speak to him and either Randee's scoop instincts immediately went into overdrive or he really didn't want to spend his vacation working on the roof. I told him not to bother to come into the office. "Get out to the motel and work from there," I said. "Have you got your camera and some film?"

"Yeah."

I told Mary to get out to Kel-Lake and work with him. Ron was developing the rest of the film we had for that day's newspaper, though we probably would not be using much of it. He and I stayed at the paper for the moment, while Randee and Mary worked the motel and the Flying W.

At that point, the men had not been brought into Carthage. I told Mary to make sure we had advance notice and we would have someone at the police station. As you might expect, by this time *The Carthage Press* had company on this story, including representatives from just about every radio and television station in the Joplin/Carthage area, and reporters from Kansas City, Tulsa, and Springfield were on their way.

But we did have a jump on the competition and this was our home area. As Randee interviewed the motel owners and the other guests, Mary Guccione was across the street at the Flying W.

This was an odd couple of reporting if ever one existed. Randee stood well over six feet, with dark black hair and a fastidiously-groomed mustache, while Mary, a woman in her late 20s, stood only four feet 11 on tiptoes, spoke with an energetic Alvin and the Chipmunks type voice, and had an appearance of looking ready for the junior prom. It didn't matter. They were both excellent reporters.

As Mary interviewed people at the Flying W, there was a feeling of relief that two of the Oklahoma City bombers had been captured, and astonishment that it happened in Carthage.

As Mary talked with everyone in sight, she was competing with the local television stations, which were passing their feeds along to the networks. The news of the arrests had people flocking to the convenience store. "It's been a crazy morning," clerk Crystil Hawkins told Mary. "I had to sneak in the backroads to get to work. I've never seen anything like it."

◆   ◆   ◆

The next stop for Robert Jacks and Gary Land was the Carthage police station and that created an immediate problem ... the facility was far too small for the attention it was about to receive.

Jim Farley had enough information to let us know the stop would only be a temporary one and that federal officials were arranging transportation for the duo.

I used the computerized filing system Ron Graber had devised for the newspaper to look up information on progress on the construction of a new police station. One of the arguments for the facility was the limited capacity of the present station and nothing proved that point more than this situation. The Carthage Police Department was under siege from the media and the public.

For a while, until I asked the receptionists to hold the calls, I was dealing with reporters from *Newsweek*, *Time*, *Associated Press*, the *New York Times*, and many lesser outlets (at least from a circulation standpoint) wanting information about the two men.

Despite the limited size of my staff, I had some resources that many small newspapers did not have. In addition to having a publisher with an unerring nose for news, we also had veteran advertising salesman Stewart Johnson, who was an excellent photographer. We were able to place two photographers, Stewart and Ron Graber, at the police station awaiting the departure of Land and Jacks. It was not going to be easy to get good photographs. Not only was the police station far too small, but the streets around it were already packed with people who were awaiting the departure of the Oklahoma City bombing suspects, or "material witnesses," as they were being called.

More than 20 media organizations were represented, including all three Joplin television stations, area radio stations, statewide and national news organizations and Carthage resident Richard Bliss, who was videotaping it for his company, Blissful Memories, which normally sold videotapes of school events, weddings, and parties.

Mayor Don Riley told me, "I would say if anything shows the need for a bigger police station in Carthage, this does." This was not the first experience the station had with a major media event. At the beginning of January 1994, only 16 months earlier, the station had not been big enough to handle the local-only media onslaught following the arrest of a Carthage man for the murder of eight-year-old Douglas Ryan Ringler. The police station was so small that older incident reports had to be kept in a trailer behind the building.

As we waited outside the station, most of the crowd was in the street, effectively keeping traffic away. I worked the crowd, doing something I have always felt was the most overused and overrated segments in newspapers and television—the man-on-the-street interview. This time was a definite exception to my philosophy.

Debbie Parker, Carthage, had been at the scene of the Connor Hotel collapse in Joplin in November 1978, when rescue workers saved a man who had been buried beneath the rubble. "Before this," she told me, "that was the biggest thing I had ever seen in person. This is something that everybody is interested in. Nobody can believe that such a thing could happen in the United States.

"And who would ever think that someone who might be involved with it would be in Carthage?"

Ms. Parker had been keeping a watchful eye, she said. "I saw the FBI going in there with two big, green bags. I don't know what was in them."

Many of those in the crowd wanted to be somewhere where a piece of history was taking place. One of those was 19-year-old Stacey Wecker, a 1994 Carthage Senior High School graduate whose high school volleyball career I had covered (I also covered a considerable amount of sports for The Press, including Carthage High School volleyball and girls basketball games, some junior high games, and some area contests.) "I just wanted to see if they really had John Doe," Stacey said. Despite the friendly conversations I was having with Ms. Parker and Stacey, there was a definite undercurrent of hate and resentment from this crowd. America had been angered by the deaths of 168 people in the Oklahoma City bombing and two of the men who might be responsible for that brutal act were only a few feet away from the crowd.

As I was talking with Stacey, one of the onlookers shouted, "They're coming out, they're coming out! I can see them!" Whatever the woman saw, it was not the FBI with Land and Jacks. It was a false alarm. The crowd was growing impatient, especially those of us who were already past their deadlines, but also those who were supposed to be somewhere else. "I've got to go back to work," Stacey said, but she didn't move an inch. "I really want to see this."

A few minutes after she said that, she received her opportunity. Everyone at 213 Lyon Street in Carthage thought they were seeing history in the making and perhaps they were.

FBI agents walked out of the building, with Land and Jacks in tow. The Carthage community, which like the rest of America had been stunned that something like the bombing could take place in our heartland, let the two suspects know what they thought of them in no uncertain terms.

"You bastards!" one man screamed at the top of his lungs, while others called them killers.

"I hope you die," one mousy, brown-haired woman who did not look capable of such a statement, shouted.

A Carthage police officer on a megaphone shouted, "Get back." His words were accompanied by the honking of horns from the federal agents' cars.

The agents quickly circled the suspects to keep the crowd from doing any harm to the men. At that point, my only concern, a selfish one, was that *The Carthage Press* capture that history in the making. The efforts to protect the suspects might keep us from getting the photos we needed … the photos which already had guaranteed that our paper would be at least two hours late in hitting the streets that afternoon … and if we did not get them, it would mean that might not sell enough papers to make that delay worthwhile.

I did not have to worry. Ron Graber and Stewart Johnson did not miss anything. Ron, the best photographer in southwest Missouri (and most other places), caught the photo that ran later that day at the top of page one of The Carthage Press—an FBI agent helping Robert Jacks into a car, surrounded by other federal agents.

It took a while for the crowd to clear enough for the motorcade to leave the station. Land and Jacks were the targets of more verbal attacks, obscene gestures, and waved fists, but no one approached the car.

After the crowd was cleared to the point where the federal motorcade could pass through, *The Carthage Press* contingent zipped back to office, which was about five blocks from the station. We had the material, now we had to write, get film developed, and somehow get our paper printed.

◆　　　◆　　　◆

In about a six-hour time period, *The Carthage Press* staff put together a newspaper that turned out to be one of our best-selling editions of all time. The entire front page was devoted to the story, with Ron's photo, along with Mary's story about the scene at the police station at the top, above the banner.

Randee Kaiser's account of the capture was featured above the fold, as well as a photo he took at the motel of law enforcement officers at work. We had four more stories and a Ron Graber photo on page three, including Mary's interviews at the Flying W, Randee's interviews with the motel owners, my account of the reaction at the police station, and my background story on the problem with the size of the police station.

An AP account of the developing story, was also included, which featured some background on the bombing. We used the back page for photos by Ron, Randee, and Stewart Johnson, including a photo of Jacks in the car, covering his face with his cap, a picture of Land and Jacks' identification, Carthage Police Chief Ed Ellefsen addressing the media, FBI agents searching Room 1 at the Kel-Lake Motel, and onlookers shouting derogatory comments and more than a few obscenities at Land and Jacks as they left the station.

It was one of the biggest stories to ever happen in Carthage ... and it was also one of the biggest wastes of time.

◆   ◆   ◆

As it turned out, neither Robert Jacks nor Gary Allen Land had anything to do with the Oklahoma City bombing, so there was no reason for them not to sign their real names on the register. The two were traveling across the country, mostly following old Route 66, staying in motels, drinking beer, and eating Bigfoot Pizza from Pizza Hut ... all on the disability checks Jacks was receiving from the federal government.

Even though it turned out not to be as big a story as we initially thought it was, the capture of Land and Jacks at the Kel-Lake Motel turned out to be one of those days that remind reporters why they got into the business in the first place. We had the chance to thoroughly cover a local story with national significance and the *Carthage Press* staff made the most of it.

(One ironic sidebar to the story, the only member of The Press news staff who was not able to participate in the coverage was our sports editor, who attended classes at Missouri Southern State College during the daytime. That sports editor was John Hacker, who has since become the best spot news reporter in this area of the state (and maybe in the whole state) working for *The Joplin Globe*, the *Joplin Daily*, and as of this writing, once more on the staff of *The Carthage Press*.)

Two years after Carthage's brief brush with fame, a bizarre coincidence put the beer-guzzling, Bigfoot pizza eating dynamic duo back in the pages of The Press. National news sources printed a story about a man named Robert Jacques (pronounced Jacks), who had visited a Cassville, Missouri, real estate office with the two men convicted in the Oklahoma City bombing case, Timothy McVeigh and Terry Nichols.

The Cassville real estate broker said he contacted federal agents after he saw the arrest of Land and Jacks on television. He also said that the Robert Jacks who was arrested in Carthage was not the man who was with McVeigh and Nichols.

The story was dropped soon thereafter, and so was Carthage's connection to the Oklahoma City bombing.

DEATH OF AN ANGEL

It was standing room only at the BYKOTA Church for an early-afternoon service that two weeks earlier no one could have ever foreseen.

I was one of those standing, leaning against a wall in the back of the church, making an estimate of the number of those who were continuing to squeeze their way into the facility, which would be replaced within a year by a larger building.

More than 500 were standing or sitting shoulder to shoulder as the time for the service approached. In the front left corner, a cluster of multi-colored balloons and groupings of flowers surrounded an 11 x 17 photo of a smiling, eight-year-old boy.

Carthage was paying its final respects to Douglas Ryan Ringer, a second grader at Hawthorne Elementary School ... and a victim in the brutal murder that robbed the city of its innocence.

◆　　　◆　　　◆

I had only been managing editor of The Carthage Press for about three weeks when Randee Kaiser returned from the police beat on a late December morning with the word that police were searching for a missing eight-year-old boy. We ran the school photo of Doug Ringler, his blond hair combed to the right and a smile on his face. It was the first of many times we ran that photo, the same photo that was placed in the front of the BYKOTA church for his funeral service.

Police knew from the beginning they were probably never going to see the boy alive, but posters were distributed all over Carthage. There were not many areas where the people didn't know Doug Ringler. If they didn't know the name, they knew the face the minute they saw the posters. They had seen Doug riding his bicycle all over town, his short legs pumping the bicycle hard because he always had more friends he wanted to see. He made a lot of friends during the few years he had.

Friends and family stayed with Norma Ringler, Doug's mother, as she awaited word. On December 28, 1993, the same day Doug was reported missing, authorities discovered the body of a young boy, burned beyond recognition in a field in Fort Scott, Kan. They had no doubt, even before forensic evidence confirmed it, that they had found Doug Ringler. "There hadn't been any reports of any other missing children at that time," Carthage Police Chief Ed Ellefsen said. "We knew it had to be him." Dental records confirmed it.

Norma Ringler was surrounded by friends when she was told by Carthage police that her little boy was never coming home. She released a statement to the media the following day. "My family and I are deeply sorrowed at the loss of my son, Doug. We will greatly miss his smile, excitement for life, good nature and outgoing personality. As a born-again Christian, I am relying upon the peace and comfort that only God can bring and am confident that Doug is with the Lord in Heaven where there is no pain or suffering. I am comforted by the fact that I will see Doug again. We want to thank the Carthage Police Department, BYKOTA Church, Leggett & Platt, friends and co-workers and the entire community of Carthage for their support, kindness, and generosity."

On the same day that Mrs. Ringler was told of her son's death, Terence W. Cupp, 31, Carthage, one of those who had helped distribute the flyers with Doug's photo, was arrested and charged with first degree murder. On Dec. 31, the police, who had suspected Cupp, a family friend, from the outset, obtained a search warrant for his car, taking evidence to the Missouri Southern State College Crime Lab.

Doug Ringler and his older brother Chris Gentry spent the night with Cupp. The boys slept in Cupp's living room. Gentry told the police Cupp had said the boys could sleep with him if they got cold. When Gentry woke up, shortly past eight o'clock the next morning, he asked, "Where's Doug?"

"He just left," Cupp said.

Cupp took Gentry to the nearby Pancake Hut for breakfast then dropped him by his house. When Chris Gentry entered, Doug was nowhere in sight. A couple of minutes before noon, Norma Ringler called the Carthage Police Department and reported her son missing.

When police questioned Terry Cupp, they quickly noticed his nervousness. At first, Cupp indicated Doug was probably just running around, the way he always did. "Norma lets him walk all over town all the time."

As the questioning continued, Cupp offered another thought. "I think he may have run away from home," but he offered no reason for the boy to have run away.

The autopsy showed the extent of Terry Cupp's brutality. Doug Ringler had been sexually assaulted, his throat had been cut, and he had been strangled.

Search warrants uncovered a map in Cupp's trashcan which showed the route he took to the place where he took Doug's body. Hair samples matching Doug's were found in Cupp's car. A gas station attendant remembered a man fitting Cupp's description putting a small amount of gasoline in a red, plastic container, the same gasoline that was used to start the fire that burned the boy's body.

A search warrant later uncovered that container in a vacant house next to property owned by Cupp's mother, Sharon Hendricks, in Hallowell, Kan.

A gas log book was found in the glove compartment of Cupp's car. Cupp voluntarily took a lie detector test, and the results of that test, though inadmissible in court, indicated Cupp was lying. Blood and semen samples had also been recovered that tied Cupp to the murder.

Because Doug Ringler's body had been discovered in Kansas, the Kansas Bureau of Investigation (KBI) was called to assist with the investigation. The KBI agent on call when the assignment came through was Bill Halvorsen ... a Carthage Senior High School graduate.

As Cupp continued to proclaim his innocence, the police called in Cupp's mother, Sharon Hendricks. "I didn't do this," he told his mother, but later in a discussion with his mother, his minister, and Joplin lawyer Terence Prigmore, Cupp started crying.

"I've done something really bad," he said in a halting voice, and he acknowledged he had sex with the eight-year-old, though he continued to insist he had not killed Doug. Cupp did everything he could to keep from making eye contact with his mother, eventually burying his face in his hands.

"Mom, I'm sorry."

Finally, with his mother and minister in the room, Terry Cupp told the police what he had done. He described, in chilling detail, how he molested the boy, murdered him and disposed of the body. Every few moments, he stopped to say something to his mother or his minister. At another point, he asked to be allowed to smoke a cigarette. Wanting to do nothing to stop the story, the police agreed to the break.

After the cigarette, he told about driving to a remote area where a cattle pen was located.

"I didn't stop," he said, "there was a farmer out there working, I had to drive on by." He drove around for a while, then circled back to the property. "I took Doug out of the car and I put him on the ground," Cupp said, "then I poured the gasoline over him," he paused, then added, "and I set him on fire."

Once the statement was finished, Terry Cupp, the man who single mother Norma Ringler thought would be a good father figure for her sons, was arrested for murder.

Cupp never said why he killed Doug Ringler, but Cupp's mother had a theory that she shared with KBI investigator Bill Halvorsen. "I think Terry had so much heartache because of his sexual desire for Doug that he might have thought killing him would get rid of the heartache."

◆   ◆   ◆

I looked at the two banners surrounding Doug Ringler's photo. Both signified that he was a "Hawthorne Hero," the highest honor a student at his elementary school could receive.

"We thank you for the eight years we had with Douglas and the impact that he had on our lives," Mike Morgan, an elder at BYKOTA Church, said. He said that no obituary could capture the qualities that endeared Doug to his friends, neighbors and second grade classmates at Hawthorne Elementary.

"His sandy, blond hair, blue eyes ... and that wonderful smile. He loved being with people. He loved his school, he loved his classmates, and he loved his church. And he was loved by all who knew him."

People on all sides of me were reacting in the same manner. Nearly everyone had tears streaming down their faces. Mine would come later when I began writing the story.

BYKOTA Church minister Michael Banes, said, "All of us have been deeply violated by this terrible tragedy. We need to choose to release Doug into the hands of the Lord and trust him to that place where there is no more suffering and no more tears. It is my hope that as a family, church and community we will remember Doug as an outgoing, friendly, energetic child that loved to be involved in all that was going on around him. Though his years were short, we all know that Doug enjoyed life to the fullest. We will miss Doug very much. We will miss his smile and the bubbly joy that his presence brought, but our hope rests in the assurance that we will see Doug again."

When the service ended, I followed the family and church members to Park Cemetery. The balloons that had surrounded his picture in the church were placed above his casket, and after a few words were spoken at his graveside, the balloons were released into the air and buffeted about by the gusting winds.

◆   ◆   ◆

Prosecutors filed documents in Jasper County Circuit Court indicating they would seek the death penalty for Terry Cupp, whose trial date was set for October 1995. Though he had had brutally murdered an eight-year-old who had never done any harm to anyone, Terry Cupp was not prepared to pay the ultimate price for his crime.

On May 16, 1995, John Bailey, the public defender for capitol crimes, who had been placed in charge of Cupp's defense, stopped by Norma Ringler's home.

"How would you feel about a plea bargain?" Bailey asked. The terms of the agreement would have Cupp receiving a life sentence without possibility of parole.

She told Bailey she would not oppose the plea bargain arrangement. "This is the best thing, not just for my family, but for the entire community," she told me shortly after she talked to the lawyer.

"Having to go through the trial would have been torture enough, but it wouldn't have ended there. If Terry had received the death penalty, we would have to go through years and years of appeals. That would have been real hard.

"And I was also worried about the trial," Mrs. Ringler said. "I didn't want to see the evidence, the pictures of my Doug. I heard they were very gruesome. That's not the picture I want to have of Doug. I want to remember Doug the way he was the last time I saw him. He was a happy, little boy, so happy, and so excited about life."

Though a year and half had passed since the murder, it was obvious that Norma Ringler had not come to grips with what had happened and she probably never would. "I just don't see how someone could have done that to Doug," she said, and though she was trying hard to fight back the tears, it was a losing battle. "I figure Terry doesn't even know why it happened. How can there be any explanation for it? I sometimes think that this has been a ploy of the devil to cause problems in this area where people have such strong faith in God.

"I just hope somehow that we can put this behind us. Vengeance won't do anyone any good. Maybe with this (the plea bargain), we can finally put Doug to rest."

Terry Cupp, the slight, bespectacled killer who robbed Carthage of its Midwestern comfort and its sense of innocence, officially entered his guilty plea May 17, 1995, in Jasper County Circuit Court. Before the plea was accepted, Judge David Darnold asked Cupp 119 questions, the same battery of questions that anyone entering a guilty plea in his court had to answer. These included questions on whether his plea was voluntary, whether he was happy with the job his lawyers had done for him, and if he understood that his plea meant he could not come back later and ask for a trial.

"With this plea, you are giving up your right to have a trial. Do you understand that?" Judge Darnold asked.

"Yes," Cupp said, answering that question as he had all of the others before it, in a thin, reedy voice that barely registered.

After Judge Darnold accepted the plea, Jasper County Prosecuting Attorney David Dally (now a circuit court judge), made a statement to the media. Asked if it bothered him that someone who had committed a crime as heinous as Cupp's was being allowed to live, Dally said, "Life in prison is not going to be a picnic for Mister Cupp. If there is one thing they do not like in prison, it is someone who hurts a child."

◆   ◆   ◆

When a person enters a guilty plea of his own volition, that should be the end of the case, but that was not the case for Terry Cupp. A few months after he was sentenced to life in prison without the possibility of parole, Cupp filed a motion in Jasper County Circuit Court, asking that his sentence be tossed out and that he be allowed to go to trial.

Though disgusted by the prospect of a reopening of Cupp's case, Carthage Police Chief Ed Ellefsen was not surprised by the motion. "They get up there and find out life isn't easy and they're going to be up there a long time, so what have they got to lose?"

Judge Darnold dismissed the motion, which was then taken to the Missouri Southern District Court of Appeals, where it was rejected on Nov. 6, 1996.

Cupp tried again on Jan. 12, 1998. In documents filed in Jasper County Circuit Court, he claimed "material evidence" had been suppressed that had an effect on his plea and deprived him of due process. He never said what the evidence was.

Cupp also charged "outrageous misconduct" by the Jasper County Prosecuting Attorney's office and the police had kept him from receiving due process. Cupp, who served as his own lawyer in filing the petition, said he would supply more information after the court appointed a lawyer for him.

His petition indicated he had witnesses who would testify about his mental condition, information he claimed was kept from him and could have invalidated the statements he made to the police when he admitted to killing Doug Ringler.

Darnold turned down Cupp once more, noting that Cupp had already filed an appeal and that court rules only allow him for file once for post-conviction relief. Once again, the killer took his case to the Southern District Court of Appeals, helped by a public defender, paid for by the taxpayers, including Norma Ringler, whose son he had brutally murdered. The court upheld Judge Darnold's ruling on Jan. 26, 1999, and Cupp remains behind bars.

◆   ◆   ◆

On May 20, 1994, Hawthorne Elementary School paid tribute to Doug Ringler with a ceremony dedicating a bench inscribed with Doug's name. The bench was placed under a tree, where it was surrounded by rose bushes and chrysanthemums. The bench and its surroundings were christened Doug's Place. "He loved nature," Hawthorne Principal Charles Paden said. A cadet teacher told Norma Ringler, "I never got to know Doug very well, but he was always bouncing around. He made school a lot less dreary.

"He was an angel."

Teacher Julie Collier's second grade class … Doug's class … made a collage of drawings for Mrs. Ringler of the good times they remembered having with Doug. All of them referred to Doug in the present tense.

"We don't talk about it much any more," Mrs. Collier said, but obviously it was still fresh in their thoughts. "They see students move in and out of here a lot and it's almost like he's moved away. They know they won't see him again, but they still remember him like he was. I don't know if any of them have ever experienced anything like this before, but I know I haven't. And you know if it's hard on the adults, then it's really hard on the kids."

After the ceremony, Mrs. Collier gave Norma Ringler a photo of Doug taken just before Christmas break, just a few days before his death. Mrs. Ringler had never seen the photo before. She looked at the photo, then she placed it next to her heart. It was the last picture that was ever taken of her son.

A few years later, when Hawthorne Elementary School closed its doors for the final time and was put on the auction block (and later torn down) Carthage R-9 school officials made sure extra care was taken with Doug's memorial bench.

At first, Kenneth Bowman, who was R-9 superintendent at the time, told me school officials considered moving the bench to Columbian Elementary, the school Doug would have attended had he lived.

Then at the request of Norma Ringler and with the cooperation of the Carthage Public Library Board, the memorial was moved to the E. L. Dale Memorial Library Gardens, where it sits a few feet away from Carthage artist Bill Snow's Alice in Wonderland statue, in an area designed for children.

School officials, library officials and Mrs. Ringler agreed that it would be the perfect place to put the bench, to make sure that Douglas Ryan Ringler, forever eight years old, will never be forgotten.

PUBLIC EDUCATION UNDER FIRE

The biggest scam being pushed in Jefferson City and Washington these days is the fiction that educational vouchers are a cure-all for what is wrong with American schools.

It would probably surprise many people to know that public schools are not in horrible shape. Most of them are not even in bad shape, and the few that are, mostly located in inner-city areas, are failing because of things that are beyond the scope of public schools, little things like drugs, violence, broken homes, and poverty.

Of course, there is room for improvement in public schools, and most public schools are not content to stand still. Each year, we add more technology, work on new methods to improve our classrooms, and provide the best education possible for our children.

So why the attack on public schools?

Obviously, there is an element of elitism to it. If you attend a private school, then naturally you are receiving a better education than a student who is attending a public school. Only studies do not come to that conclusion. For the most part, unbiased studies have indicated that public school students fare about the same on tests as do those who attend private schools.

If the educational value is about the same, then why should we be pushing our students toward private schools? The reason, as with nearly all things in politics, can be traced to money.

When different industries have been deregulated, some successfully, some not, big business has been lurking in the background waiting to cash in. It is the same with education. If that were not the case, then how else could you explain the continued existence of Edison Schools?

Edison, the brainchild of Channel One creator Chris Whittle, has never made a cent. It has lost money in every year of its existence, yet it continues to attract investors.

Why?

The answer to that one is easy. Check the language of No Child Left Behind which almost forces schools that do not meet the act's artificial barriers to hire private firms to run certain aspects of a school at the first stage, and later the entire school. Edison is in on the ground floor and stands to swoop in like a vulture to grab up the remnants of public schools, some of which will fail because they have one subgroup fail to improve on standardized tests.

No Child Left Behind, just as its supporters knew it would, has created a whole new group of businesses, designing everything from Edison-type business management of public schools to virtual schools and each year state legislatures are being pressured to cave in and abandon the public schools so parents will have "school choice."

The businesses want this to happen so they can cash in on it. If you need any further proof of how much money can be made from school vouchers, simply check the financial contributions politicians are receiving from voucher supporters.

Leading the push for educational vouchers in Missouri is the prince of privilege Governor Matt Blunt. On Aug. 5, 2005, our governor was the keynote speaker at the national convention of All Children Matter, a pro-voucher group founded by former Amway president and unsuccessful candidate for governor of Michigan Dick DeVos. Traveling to Colorado to speak at the convention was the least the governor could do since it was All Children Matter who put him in the governor's mansion (at least for the two or three days each week that he stays there).

In the waning days of the 2004 gubernatorial campaign, All Children Matter poured $196,252 into radio advertising blasting Blunt's opponent, State Auditor Claire McCaskill. That ad blitz likely provided the razor-thin margin by which Blunt became the second youngest governor (next to Kit Bond) in Missouri's history.

During his three years as governor, Blunt has made four appointments to the State Board of Education, the governing body for public schools. All four have been voucher supporters, even though one, Donayle Whitmore-Smith, had her nomination withdrawn before it was taken up by the Senate.

The governor's first nomination was a wolf in sheep's clothing. Debi Demien was promoted as a former public schoolteacher and director of marketing for Demien Construction. Mrs. Demien was appointed to the board in March 2006. While it was noted that she was involved in the family business, Demien Construction, what wasn't noted is that she is director of marketing for the company's Building God's Way division, which builds churches and Christian schools. Any sort of movement of public money into private schools will obviously benefit Mrs. Demien.

Eight years ago, she wrote a book entitled *Stealing America, the National Takeover of the Economy, Education and State Governments*, which primarily criticizes the school-to-work programs being used in public schools. She is an outspoken critic of Missouri's A+ program, which allows students involved in the program to receive free schooling at Missouri community colleges.

In 1996, Mrs. Demien was an Alan Keyes delegate to the National Republican Convention. These are Keyes' thoughts on education, taken from a February 2002 commentary:

"Vouchers will help children and families, just as school choice has benefited those pursuing higher education. The educational benefit of choosing schools for reasons of instructional quality, instead of economic necessity, are obvious. Voucher programs also end the "double taxation" many families face—paying for public schools through their taxes, and yet also paying to send their children to non-public institutions. Parental choice will also increase parental involvement. When parents think that education is the government's business, they tend to leave it to the so-called professional educators. But having chosen a school, and personally directed the dollars that pay for their child's attendance there, more parents will understand that their role in learning should not be passive. The natural motive to evaluate and assist a service we have chosen and purchased provides an important additional impetus for parental involvement. Vouchers will broaden participation in access to quality education. After decades of national fretting about unequal access, sometimes with racial overtones that have nothing to do with education, will we reject this simple solution to the plight of those—particularly in the inner city—who simply do not have access to any but failed, monopolistic public-school systems?"

What has also not been mentioned about Mrs. Demien has been her role as president of "Restoring America." The organization's website talks about a war of values being taught in America:

"Dr. James Dobson of 'Focus on the Family' has repeatedly stated that we are engaged in 'a Civil War of values' in our culture, and the prize is our children.

He wrote—'Children are the prize to the winners of the second great civil war. Those who control what young people are taught and what they experience—what they see, hear, think, and believe—will determine the future course for the nation. Given that influence, the predominant value system of an entire culture can be overhauled in one generation, or certainly in two, by those with unlimited access to children.'"

Or this quote:

"... this is supposed to be a Constitutional Republic—based entirely upon Christian principles—with no separation of Church and State. Since our very form of government and legal system were formed from, and based on, God's natural law and the Bible, then how can we separate church from State? We cannot. The heart cannot be removed from the body without the death of that body. Unfortunately and to our shame, none of this is being taught in our schools today. We will either educate our children to be the enemies of freedom and independence—as we are currently doing—or, we can educate them in the truths and visions of our Founding Fathers—raising future patriots for America."

The *Restoring America* site proudly reprints an article entitled "On the sin of sending kids to public schools," which talks about the book *The Harsh Truth About Public Schools*. The article includes the following passage:

"In the book, Shortt documents the pitfalls of public schools, saying the anti-Christian thrust of the governmental school system produces inevitable results: 'moral relativism (no fixed standards), academic dumbing down, far-left programs, near absence of discipline and the persistent but pitiable rationalizations offered by government education professionals.'

"Shortt also urges pastors to read the book so they might 'understand why the church can no longer abdicate its historic role in the education of our children.'

"Says Short: 'The Harsh Truth About Public Schools' makes it clear why no Christian child should be left behind in government schools. Our Christian children are perishing because parents and pastors lack knowledge. The information in this book exposes the 'salt and light' and the 'our schools are different' rationalizations for educating Christian children in pagan schools for the contemptible falsehoods they are.

"Any parent or pastor who genuinely desires to be faithful in the education of Christian children needs to find out what the public schools are actually doing, rather than relying on what they are saying they are doing or on memories of the public schools as they may have existed 10, 20 or 30 years ago."

As for "reforming" the public schools, the article posted so prominently on Mrs. Demien's organization's website offers the following:

"But what about reforming the public schools? Isn't that a solution?

"Responds Shortt: 'Public schools cannot be reformed to provide a Christian education, and the evidence is overwhelming that even conventional secular reforms to reinstate traditional academic and moral standards will continue to fail. But even if you think that we should nevertheless try to reinstate traditional academic and moral standards in the schools, taking your children out is the most effective thing you can do to help the children whose parents have left them behind in the public schools. Only the threat of a collapse of the entire public school system offers even the remotest prospect of positive change. Traditional reform efforts are a waste of time."

According to documents on file with the Missouri Secretary of State's office, *Restoring America* is owned by Mrs. Demien and Richard Vieth of St. Charles. This was Governor Matt Blunt's first choice to serve on the board regulating public schools—a woman whose own websites indicate she does not believe in public schools?

◆   ◆   ◆

In October 2006, Blunt topped the appointment of Debi Demien by announcing his second choice for the school board—Donayle Whitmore-Smith of St. Louis. Unlike Mrs. Demien, who at least had served as a public school-teacher, Ms. Whitmore-Smith was a product of private schools, having founded an unsuccessful one and having attended private schools for almost of all of K-12 education ... and the one time she enrolled in a public school, for just a short time, it was a horrible experience for her. Out of thousands of people who were actually qualified for the job, this was Matt Blunt's idea of who should be in charge of public education.

Ms. Whitmore-Smith created the Ptah Academy, a St. Louis private school.

An Oct. 16, 2001, article in the *St. Louis Post-Dispatch* described the beginning of the day at the academy. "The ribbons of incense and the children who meditate beneath them at the start of each school day leave no doubt that the Ptah Academy of Arts and Sciences isn't your typical school."

The academy is named after an ancient Egyptian god and "includes of elements of ancient spiritualism in its instruction," according to the Post-Dispatch article, which continued, "The school is not religious, Whitmore said, but it does encourage children to tap into their 'spiritual energy.'"

The article indicated the school included "yoga, organic meals, tai chi and daily 'inner studies' or sessions of meditation" in its curriculum.

In a February 2005 article in the pro-voucher publication *School Reform News*, Ms. Whitmore-Smith said that she had attended private schools until high school and her experience at a public school was "hell." Ms. Whitmore-Smith said, "Academically, it just couldn't match what I'd been getting (in private schools)."

Ms. Whitmore-Smith was one of the leading proponents of unsuccessful pro-voucher legislation that was considered in 2006 in the Missouri General Assembly.

After *The Turner Report* got the ball rolling, the media jumped all over the Donayle Whitmore-Smith appointment. An article in the Nov. 22, 2006, Post-Dispatch noted, "For the past five years, she has headed an effort called School Choice Missouri, a campaign aimed at raising awareness about options such as charter schools, vouchers and tax-credit scholarships. The initiative is funded by the Milton and Rose D. Friedman Foundation, an Indiana-based group that advocates for public vouchers."

Governor Blunt's chief of staff Ed Martin told the Post-Dispatch that any thought that Ms. Whitmore-Smith would be anti-public education is ridiculous:

"If we thought that, she wouldn't be on the state board of education, because the governor is committed to public education," Martin said.

It should be noted that before becoming Blunt's chief of staff Martin served as attorney and treasurer for All Children Matter in Missouri.

Incorporation papers filed Oct. 22, 2004 linked Ms. Whitmore-Smith with a who's who of voucher proponents.

In the papers, filed in connection with the incorporation of the Missouri Coalition for School Choice, Inc., Ms. Whitmore-Smith was listed as the incorporator. The registered agent and corporation chairman is St. Louis attorney Mark D. Mittleman, a maximum contributor to Matt Blunt's 2004 campaign, as well as to the campaign of Lt. Gov. Peter Kinder.

Other board members included:

—James Cooper, Ballwin: executive director of Missouri Council for Private Education

—George Henry: superintendent of Catholic education for the Archdiocese of St. Louis

—Rabbi Mark Kalish: executive director of Agudath Israel of America Midwest Region, who is quoted in one newspaper account as saying that whether a candidate supports vouchers is a make-or-break issue (with the rabbi clearly favoring vouchers).

—Edward R. Martin, Jr. St. Louis, the governor's chief of staff

—Joshua Scheiderer: The address listed for Scheiderer in the incorporation papers, 4500 Little Blue Parkway, Independence, is the address of a combination Christian church and private school.

—David Waterman, St. Louis: Waterman is director of Lutheran Schools in St. Louis.

The secretary of state's records indicate Missouri Coalition for School Choice, Inc., dissolved in January 2006. According to the incorporation papers: "Upon the dissolution of the corporation, the board of directors shall, after paying or making provision for the payment of all of the liabilities of the corporation, distribute all the assets of the corporation to Alliance for School Choice of Phoenix, Arizona."

Alliance for School Choice is one of the most powerful pro-voucher groups in the United States. We will be talking about the group more a little later in this chapter.

In a guest column in the Jan. 18, 2006, *St. Louis American*, Ms. Whitmore Smith indicated that if the late civil rights leader Dr. Martin Luther King were still alive, he would be a voucher proponent. She wrote:

"But what is most troubling is the amount of energy we spend talking about our education problems. Dr. King was a man of action. In his time, people rolled up their sleeves and created solutions for the community's issues. We constantly keep discussing reforming the school district, building better educational facilities, balancing the budget, but what about educating the children? As well as raising the scores of black and brown children who come from impoverished conditions and whose families have little resources or opportunities? It's a known fact that you have a choice of schools for your children, if you have money. I'm confident that Dr. King would have wanted us to focus on empowering individuals, not marrying ourselves to systems. His message was about consistent change and growth to become real stakeholders in America. We will not see that level of growth collectively, if we continue to do things the same way. It is a tragedy that the mental murder of thousands of black children is occurring across America as we speak and we waste our time arguing over the delivery mechanisms."

Eventually, the opposition of the state senator from Ms. Whitmore-Smith's district, Jeff Smith, D-St. Louis, caused the governor to pull her appointment, but he had another voucher supporter all ready to go.

◆   ◆   ◆

Of Governor Blunt's four appointments to the State Board of Education, Rev. Stanley Archie, Kansas City, has come to the closest to being someone who could actually advocate for public schools, but even Rev. Archie has a pro-voucher background.

At a news conference, Archie, a former private school teacher and administrator, expressed his support for programs that give parents alternatives to public schools. "I do believe in a competitive market when it comes to education," he said.

However, in an interview with reporter Janese Heavin of the *Columbia Daily Tribune* and in an e-mail to me, Archie denied that he was a voucher supporter. This passage was included in Ms. Heavin's article:

"Archie told the Tribune this morning that he does not support using tax dollars for private or religious schools.

"'I do not support the idea of using vouchers,' he said. 'To use tax dollars for private purposes compromises the general philosophy of why we have tax dollars in the first place.'

"Archie said he comes from a family of public schoolteachers and principals and believes "strongly in public education." He also said he has tried to separate himself from Whitmore-Smith, whom he has never met but has been tied to because of the close timing of the nominations. Archie said he has no problem with families choosing to send their children to private schools, 'but that doesn't negate the responsibility to public education … to pay for and support the public school system.'"

In his e-mail to me, Archie emphasized that he was "a strong supporter of public schools."

◆   ◆   ◆

The governor's fourth appointment to the State Board was former Rep. Derio Gambaro, who is currently seated on the board despite not having his appointment approved by the Senate. Blunt made a recess appointment, giving the voucher supporter eight months in office before the Senate is back in session in January 2008.

After the governor appointed Gambaro in June, Ms. Heavin, the best education reporter in the state, quickly noted the former representative's pro-voucher tendencies.

"Gambaro served in the Missouri House of Representatives from 1998 to 2002 and unsuccessfully ran for the Senate last year. His 2006 campaign was padded by a more than $9,000 donation from All Children Matter, a Michigan-based pro-voucher organization.

"Gambaro is also on the board of directors of the Children's Education Alliance of Missouri, a school choice organization based in Columbia."

A quick check of Missouri Ethics Commission documents shows that Gambaro's unsuccessful bid for the Democratic nomination for a state senate seat in

2005 was almost entirely bankrolled by retired billionaire Rex Sinquefield, the head of the conservative pro-voucher Show-Me Institute. Though a contribution limit of $675 was in effect at that time, Sinquefield contributed $20,700 into Gambaro's account during its final quarter, by placing $6,500 donations into three committee accounts, which then turned the money over to Gambaro. No pretense was made otherwise, since those were the only contributions those committees received during that time period. Sinquefield and his wife each chipped in with $600 directly to Gambaro to account for the other $1,200. Despite the big bucks, Gambaro finished third in a five-way race to Jeff Smith, the same senator who blocked Donayle Whitmore-Smith's nomination and will have to approve Gambaro in January.

◆　　　◆　　　◆

As I mentioned earlier, one of the biggest reasons politicians are attracted to the pro-voucher movement is the massive amount of money it brings to campaigns. During the brief period at the beginning of 2007 when campaign contributions were lifted in Missouri, the so-called "school choice" movement poured big bucks into Missourians for Matt Blunt, the governor's campaign committee. Blunt's first quarter disclosure form, filed with the Missouri Ethics Commission, shows that three of the governor's biggest contributors were voucher supporters.

Ethics Commission documents show Sinquefield, the head of the conservative Show-Me Institute, contributed $100,000 to Blunt on March 14. The Show-Me Institute is one of the leading advocates for vouchers. Sinquefield has funded studies to prove vouchers would be the proper path for Missouri education to take.

But Sinquefield's $100,000 contribution in March was not the only one of that amount received by Blunt, according to the Ethics Commission documents. He also received $100,000 each from EthelMae Humphreys and David Humphreys, the mother and son who are in charge of TAMKO in Joplin.

Mrs. Humphreys sits on the board of directors of two powerful pro-voucher groups, the CATO Institute and Sinquefield's Show-Me Institute.

A quick examination of the Cato Institute website makes the point clear:

"We envision a day when state-run schools give way to a dynamic independent system of schools competing to meet the needs of every American child."

The titles of the books and articles funded by the CATO Institute leave no doubt about where it stands on education:

—School Choice: Sunshine Replaces the Clouds
—Voucher Wars: Waging the Legal Battle Over School Choice
—Educational Freedom in Urban America
—What Americans Can Learn About School Choice from Other Countries

If the $300,000 Blunt received from the Humphreys and Sinquefield wasn't enough, the governor also received a $25,000 donation from the CNS Corporation, run by millionaire Charles Norval Sharpe, who runs the Heartland Academy, a private school, and has long been a backer of pouring public money into private schools.

It was Sharpe's private plane that was used earlier this year to taxi Matt Blunt across the state for a victory lap when he signed a bill to sell off Missouri college loans.

◆   ◆   ◆

The attack on public education is not limited to the executive branch in Missouri by any means. The most anti-public education legislator in Missouri, Rep. Jane Cunningham, R-Chesterfield, was chosen by Speaker of the House Rod Jetton to serve as chairman of the House Education Committee.

Ms. Cunningham is a top official in the American Legislative Exchange Council (ALEC), and at one of that organization's meetings in August 2005 in Grapevine, Texas, she criticized benefit packages for teachers, including pensions. At the meeting, she led a discussion over the 65 percent proposal, a misleading proposal that would require schools to put at least 65 percent of their funding into the classroom, but fails to include such items as libraries and school nurses in the 65 percent, and how it might be impacted by teacher benefits, according to the Hernando, Fla., Classroom Teachers Association website.

"Chair Jane Cunningham seized on this, suggesting that legislators could 'define it (65 percent solution) a little tighter' to exclude pensions or other benefits from spending on classrooms—in other words: driving down spending for teachers and staff."

That representation of the way Rep. Cunningham feels about public school-teachers comes from what appears to be what some of our GOP legislators would refer to as a liberal website.

However, an even more illuminating picture of Rep. Cunningham's true views about public education comes from an Oct. 1, 2003, article in the conservative *School Reform News*.

Under the headline, "Trying to Make a Difference in the Show-Me State," the article tells the story of how Ms. Cunningham came to favor vouchers following her experiences as a school board member. When she tried to do something about parents taking their children out of public school and placing them in private school, she said, she ran into a lack of interest. "We have fewer children to educate and we still get their taxes," she says her fellow board members told her. She said that with her background in economics she could see the harm this education "monopoly" was causing. Ms. Cunningham's story seems questionable since Missouri schools are paid by the average daily attendance, meaning that her school lost money for every student who decided to transfer to a private school. Of course, a *School Reform News* reporter would hardly be the one who would question Ms. Cunningham on that point.

The point was further driven home, she said, after she took one of her sons out of public school (the article does not say why) and put him in a Catholic school. Her son, who had been receiving A's and B's in math in public school, did poorly in the private school.

"The staff at the Catholic school thought he must have a learning disability, because they could not imagine his local school had done such a poor job," Rep. Cunningham said.

The article goes on to say that "after intensive personal attention by his teacher, her son rose to the 90th percentile in math."

Rep. Cunningham makes no bones about her efforts to move Missouri toward a voucher system. The *School Reform News* article says, "In 2003, Cunningham sponsored two school choice bills, both designed 'to get folks comfortable with the concept.' One bill addressed the issue of access to programs in public schools denied to non-public schoolchildren whose families were residing in and paying taxes to the public schools. The other, HB 345, would have given school choice to at-risk children in low-income families and in families where a parent is a prison inmate. Although neither bill passed, she was happy to be able to bring some Black Caucus members on board with HB 345." The magazine article was written by Laura J. Swartley, communications director for the Milton and Rose Friedman Foundation, Indianapolis, Ind. The Friedman Foundation began the school voucher movement in 1955.

Rep. Cunningham is serving as chairman of the ALEC Education Task Force. Her co-chairman is Robert Enlow of the same Milton & Rose Friedman Foundation. In 2006, The Friedman Foundation hired a lobbyist to represent its interests in Missouri … Andrew Blunt, the governor's brother (though the younger Blunt is no longer the lobbyist for the organization).

Rep. Cunningham created quite a stir at the beginning of 2005 with a multi-page letter she wrote asking to be reappointed chairman of the House Education Committee. One of her selling points was the amount of money she had brought into Republican politicians' campaigns from All Children Matter.

Each year for the past few years, efforts have been made to pass a so-called "tuition tax credit bill" which would give public money to students in failing school districts in St. Louis to attend private schools. It has been widely seen as a way to open the door for vouchers.

The bill would create a tax credit that would encourage people and corporations to donate to new education scholarship foundations. Under the bill, 65 percent of a donation would be reimbursed, in the form of reduced taxes. The privately run foundations would then award scholarships averaging $5,000 to students who currently attend one of the 13 school districts in Missouri that lack full state accreditation due to low performance.

An article in the *St. Louis Post-Dispatch* quoted Rep. Ed Robb, R-Columbia, as saying that he hoped to convince rural legislators, who have opposed previous incarnations of this bill of his bill's value.

According to Missouri Ethics Commission documents, All Children Matter paid $9,679.32 to support Ed Robb's candidacy in 2006 ... and paid for $24,710.59 worth of negative advertising against Robb's Democratic opponent, former Columbia Public Schools Superintendent Jim Ritter. That was probably the difference in the race, which Robb won by a handful of votes.

One of the co-sponsors of HB 498 was Rep. Dwight Scharnhorst, R-Valley Park. All Children Matter spent $3,338.24 to support Scharnhorst, and paid $6,355.42 to attack Scharnhorst's opponent.

All Children Matter spent $31,640 supporting co-sponsor Rodney Hubbard, D-St. Louis. The co-sponsor list also included Rep. Jane Cunningham, who as noted earlier campaigned for her position as chairman of the House Elementary and Secondary Education Committee by writing a letter to Speaker Rod Jetton, R-Marble Hill, bragging about how much funding she brought to House Republicans from All Children Matter. Jetton, too, was a recipient of a maximum $325 contribution from the organization, as were most of the bill's co-sponsors.

Joplin area co-sponsors, Marilyn Ruestman, R-Joplin, Ed Emery, R-Lamar, and Steve Hunter, R-Joplin, all received maximum contributions from All Children Matter.

If there is any doubt as to the true intent of the Robb bill, it should be erased by the title given to it—the Milton Friedman 'Put Parents in Charge' Education Program. Mr. Friedman, who died in 2006, is widely known as the father of the voucher movement. He created the concept in the 1950s and has helped push it over the years through the Friedman Foundation, the same group which for most of 2006 had Andrew Blunt serving as its lobbyist.

The bill failed by a 96-62 vote, but its proponents say it will return in the 2008 legislative session. The well-financed pro-voucher movement continues to build strength in the state by forming a coalition between conservative Republicans and some African American Democrats.

In June, House Speaker Pro Tem Carl Bearden, R-St. Charles, resigned from the House to form a new lobbying group, Pelopidas, LLD, with Travis Brown and his wife Rachel Keller Brown. Over a two-day period in April 2007, Travis Brown spent $2,872 entertaining and wining and dining some of the top pro-voucher politicians in the state of Missouri, including Governor Matt Blunt's chief of staff Ed Martin, Bearden, and St. Louis Democrats Theodore Hoskins and Rodney Hubbard.

Though the Missouri Ethics Commission reports are not specific, they do indicate that Brown treated those politicians, as well as Rep. Kenny Jones, R-California, Rep. Dwight D. Scharnhorst, R-Manchester, Robert Knodell, an aide to Bearden, and Lucy LePage, an aide to Rep. Jane Cunningham, R-Chesterfield, to baseball games on Saturday, April 14, and Sunday, April 15, according to Brown's April disclosure report filed with the Missouri Ethics Commission. The St. Louis Cardinals played the Milwaukee Brewers that weekend.

Cardinal party suites cost $82 per ticket, according to the baseball team's website. On Sunday, April 15, all of the politicians received $164 in entertainment from Brown—the price of two tickets to the Cardinals' party suites.

In those suites, according to the team's website, Budweiser and Bud Light are served starting at 30 minutes before the ballgame and ending in the middle of the eighth inning, meals are catered, and the social area is "climate-controlled."

According to Brown's disclosure report, the only ones who did not receive $164 for entertainment, and $150 for "meals, food, and beverage," were the two assistants and Hubbard. Knodell received $82 for entertainment, apparently, the price of a game ticket, while Ms. LePage received $75 for meals, food and beverage. Hubbard was the top recipient of Brown's gifts, on April 15, receiving $328 for entertainment, and $300 for meals, food, and beverage.

While all of those listed above received Sunday, April 15, contributions, Brown's disclosure form indicates Bearden, Kenny Jones, and the two assistants were the only ones who attended Saturday's game.

On the same day that Brown filed paperwork with the Missouri Ethics Commission to represent Pelopidas, he also officially became the lobbyist for Rex Sinquefield, the principal force behind the Show-Me Institute, which has made vouchers its top priority.

In addition to Brown and Bearden, Pelopidas will be led by Brown's wife, lobbyist Rachel Keller Brown, whose sole client is Advocates for School Choice, the Phoenix, Ariz., organization that does exactly what its name says. Advocates for School Choice is the lobbying arm of the Alliance for School Choice, also based in Phoenix. Before becoming Governor Blunt's chief of staff, Ed Martin was Missouri coordinator for the Alliance for School Choice, as well as being treasurer for All Children Matter.

The odd combination of Democrats and Republicans that Brown has been wining and dining over the past few months, has almost exclusively been politicians who have favored educational vouchers and efforts to fund scholarships for students to attend private schools. Many of those politicians have also been the beneficiaries of Sinquefield's generosity, according to Ethics Commission records, including:

—Governor Matt Blunt, $100,000 (no gifts from Brown, but obviously plenty from Sinquefield)

—Rep. Talibdin El-Amin, D-St. Louis, $40,000

—Sen. Luann Ridgeway, R-Smithville, $40,000

—Rep. Rodney Hubbard, D-St. Louis, $30,000

—Rep. Ted Hoskins, D-St. Louis $10,000

—Sen. Rob Mayer, R-Dexter, $7,500

—Rep. Tim Jones, R-Eureka, $500

—Rep. Jane Cunningham, R-Chesterfield, $5,000 (only her aide received gifts from Brown, according to the Ethics Commission documents)

Make no doubt about it, public education is under attack in the state of Missouri. Even some moves that have been made that have no apparent link to the voucher movement are simple baby steps in that direction.

One such victory for the "school choice" proponents is the newly-created virtual school. The pro-business groups who are seeking to privatize public schools (while they disingenuously use religious schools as a kind of smokescreen) have been in the forefront of forming companies to provide curriculum for virtual schools, which have become the rage across the United States.

The benefits that can be provided by a virtual school are undeniable. Students who are confined to home can keep up with their studies via computer. Students whose schools do not offer certain classes can take them online.

But in state after state as voucher supporters attempt to gain a foothold, one of the steps they recommend is the creation of a virtual school. In Missouri, a Florida-based business, Connections Academy, is running the virtual elementary school and providing its curriculum.

The lobbyist for Connections Academy is Mark Dawes. He is registered to represent two clients in Missouri, Connections Academy and Advocates for School Choice.

The other lobbyist for Advocates for School Choice is Rachel Keller Brown, whose newly formed group, Pelopidas, LLC, will lead the battle for vouchers in the 2008 General Assembly.

And, as this book is being revised for publication, former House Speaker Pro Tem Carl Bearden, who just resigned from the House to work as a lobbyist with the Browns, has registered to lobby for Rex Sinquefield.

◆   ◆   ◆

Is it any wonder that problems in public education grow when it is expedient for politicians to attack it in order to bring in big bucks from Rex Sinquefield and All Children Matter?

They have made it far easier for people to belittle the work teachers do. You have those who claim teachers work one year, and then repeat their lesson plans year after year until they retire.

You have others who talk about how little work teachers do. After all, they have three months off in the summer, they don't work weekends, they get two weeks off for Christmas and a week for spring break, and they don't have to go to work when there's snow or ice on the roads.

At one time, teachers were among the most respected people in the community, and to some extent, that is still the case, but years of undermining public schools and public schoolteachers by selfish, self-serving politicians are finally taking their toll.

So let's take a look at the truth about teachers:

Yes, there are a few who use the same lesson plans year after year, but those are the exception, not the rule. Most teachers look for ways to improve their lesson plans, trying new techniques, adding technology, or using the latest educational research to improve their results. During those three-month summer vacations, many teachers are attending seminars or taking classes aimed at improving themselves and therefore the quality of the instruction they offer to their students.

One thing the politicians' constant sniping at the "failures" of public schools (most of the schools are not failing, but you would never know that from listening to the rhetoric being offered by voucher supporters) has done is to give the impression that teachers are slackers who are living off the public trough. While there are teachers who fall short, the push for "qualified teachers" fails to take into account other factors that are playing much greater roles in the scores of students who are not making the grade, including:

—Students who come from broken homes, homes in which they are exposed to drug and alcohol abuse, and homes where the children are victims of physical, emotional, and sexual abuse.

—Students who come from homes where there are no books, only the ever-constant presence of television and the Internet.

—Politicians who rip public education and then demand that the schools handle all of society's ills, whether they be sex education, information on alcohol and drugs, and personal finance information (which has become necessary thanks to politicians' coddling of those in the banking, credit card, and payday loan industries). Every time a politician adds something to the school's schedule, it takes away from the three R's that they say should be our focus.

—Fears that students, teachers, and administrators have each time they hear of another school shooting incident

—Students who simply do not care whether they learn

I am so tired of the argument that teachers knew how much money they were going to get paid so they have no business complaining about it. It is true to some extent; we do know we are not going to become wealthy from teaching, but at the same time, do we ever accept that type of talk when it comes to other public servants, such as police officers and firemen? Obviously, those are high risk, stressful occupations, but nearly every study of stressful occupations puts teaching right at or near the top. Teachers who care about the success of their students (and I have only met a handful who do not fit into that category) agonize over the ones who are failing, the ones who are having problems at home or at school, even the ones who seem to resist everything we try and have no interest whatsoever in school.

Most teachers are not 7:30 to 3 people who take off for home the second the last bell rings. Many teachers work with children after school, sponsor activities (some of which they are reimbursed for, but many of which they are not) and work on lesson plans and grading long after they have taught their final classes for the day. We do have 50-minute planning periods, but much of that time is devoted to dealing with parents and grading papers. I know of very few teachers who do not do a great deal of work at home. It's part of the job. For the most part, we don't go around talking about it, but with the constant belittling that seems to be the norm these days, somebody has to tell the story.

Most teachers are in the business because they truly love to work with children and help pave the road for their students' later success. As long as politicians and sensation-seeking media (i.e. John Stossel) take a handful of public school failures and make them appear to be commonplace instead of describing them accurately as the aberrations they truly are, we will continue to see the kind of anti-teacher sentiment that has grown over the past few years.

As long as self-serving politicians are willing to take those rare failures and use them as an excuse to open the door for vouchers and tuition tax credits, we are in danger of putting a torch to American public schools, the most successful experiment in the history of education.

When that happens, you can forget about No Child Left Behind. The children left behind will number in the millions.

978-0-595-46750-1
0-595-46750-4